INTRODUCING
ISSUES
WITH

OPPOSING VIEWPOINTS®

GANGS

INTRODUCING
ISSUES
WITH

OPPOSING VIEWPOINTS®

GANGS

Other books in the Introducing Issues
with Opposing Viewpoints series:

INTRODUCING ISSUES WITH

OPPOSING VIEWPOINTS®

GANGS

Scott Barbour, *Book Editor*

Bruce Glassman, *Vice President*
Bonnie Szumski, *Publisher, Series Editor*
Helen Cothran, *Managing Editor*

OPPOSING
VIEWPOINTS®
SERIES

GREENHAVEN PRESS
An imprint of Thomson Gale, a part of The Thomson Corporation

THOMSON
™
GALE

Detroit • New York • San Francisco • San Diego • New Haven, Conn. • Waterville, Maine • London • Munich

For more information, contact
Greenhaven Press
27500 Drake Rd.
Farmington Hills, MI 48331-3535
Or you can visit our Internet site at http://www.gale.com

LIBRARY OF CONGRESS CATALOGING-IN-PUBLICATION DATA

Gangs / Scott Barbour, book editor.
    p. cm. — (Introducing issues with opposing viewpoints)
  Includes bibliographical references and index.
  ISBN 0-7377-3221-0 (lib. : alk. paper)
  1. Gangs—United States. 2. Violence—United States. 3. United States—Social conditions. 4. Gangs. I. Barbour, Scott, 1963– . II. Series.
  HV6439.U5.G3577 2006
  364.1'06'60973—dc22

                                                        2005040395

Printed in the United States of America

CONTENTS

Indulging in a wide spectrum of ideas, beliefs, and perspectives is a critical cornerstone of democracy. After all, it is often debates over differences of opinion, such as whether to legalize abortion, how to treat prisoners, or when to enact the death penalty that shape our society and drive it forward. Such diversity of thought is frequently regarded as the hallmark of a healthy and civilized culture. As the Reverend Clifford Schutjer of the First Congregational Church in Mansfield, Ohio, declared in a 2001 sermon, "Surrounding oneself with only like-minded people, restricting what we listen to or read only to what we find agreeable is irresponsible. Refusing to entertain doubts once we make up our minds is a subtle but deadly form of arrogance." With this advice in mind, Introducing Issues with Opposing Viewpoints books aim to open readers' minds to the critically divergent views that comprise our world's most important debates.

Introducing Issues with Opposing Viewpoints simplifies for students the enormous and often overwhelming mass of material now available via print and electronic media. Collected in every volume is an array of opinions that capture the essence of a particular controversy or topic. Introducing Issues with Opposing Viewpoints books embody the spirit of nineteenth-century journalist Charles A. Dana's axiom: "Fight for your opinions, but do not believe that they contain the whole truth, or the only truth." Absorbing such contrasting opinions teaches students to analyze the strength of an argument and compare it to its opposition. From this process readers can inform and strengthen their own opinions, or be exposed to new information that will change their minds. Introducing Issues with Opposing Viewpoints is a mosaic of different voices. The authors are statesmen, pundits, academics, journalists, corporations, and ordinary people who have felt compelled to share their experiences and ideas in a public forum. Their words have been collected from newspapers, journals, books, speeches, interviews, and the Internet, the fastest growing body of opinionated material in the world.

Introducing Issues with Opposing Viewpoints shares many of the well-known features of its critically acclaimed parent series, Opposing Viewpoints. The articles are presented in a pro/con format, allowing readers to absorb divergent perspectives side by side. Active reading questions preface each viewpoint, requiring the student to approach the material thoughtfully and carefully. Useful charts, graphs, and cartoons supplement each article. A thorough introduction provides readers with crucial background on an issue. An annotated bibliography points the reader toward articles, books, and Web sites that contain additional information on the topic. An appendix of organizations to contact contains a wide variety of charities, nonprofit organizations, political groups, and private enterprises that each hold a position on the issue at hand. Finally, a comprehensive index allows readers to locate content quickly and efficiently.

Introducing Issues with Opposing Viewpoints is also significantly different from Opposing Viewpoints. As the series title implies, its presentation will help introduce students to the concept of opposing viewpoints, and learn to use this material to aid in critical writing and debate. The series' four-color, accessible format makes the books attractive and inviting to readers of all levels. In addition, each viewpoint has been carefully edited to maximize a reader's understanding of the content. Short but thorough viewpoints capture the essence of an argument. A substantial, thought-provoking essay question placed at the end of each viewpoint asks the student to further investigate the issues raised in the viewpoint, compare and contrast two authors' arguments, or consider how one might go about forming an opinion on the topic at hand. Each viewpoint contains sidebars that include at-a-glance information and handy statistics. A Facts About section located in the back of the book further supplies students with relevant facts and figures.

Following in the tradition of the Opposing Viewpoints series, Greenhaven Press continues to provide readers with invaluable exposure to the controversial issues that shape our world. As John Stuart Mill once wrote: "The only way in which a human being can make some approach to knowing the whole of a subject is by hearing what can be said about it by persons of every variety of opinion and studying all modes in which it can be looked at by every character of mind. No wise man ever acquired his wisdom in any mode but this." It is to this principle that Introducing Issues with Opposing Viewpoints books are dedicated.

INTRODUCTION

"For the inner-city youth, the gang provides for the most basic need: survival in a dangerous environment."
—George L. Howell, *Raising Black and Biracial Children*

Many factors are offered to explain why teenagers—and even preteens—join gangs. Gang experts typically cite a list of causes, including peer pressure, poverty, a craving for excitement, and a desire to make money, earn respect, and attract girlfriends or boyfriends. This catalog of causes suggests that it is difficult to pinpoint the exact reason any individual joins a gang. Rather, any given young person most likely joins a gang for any number of reasons. However, despite the difficulty in ascribing an exact cause, a few major themes are evident in most discussions of why youths join gangs. One common theme is a need for belonging and protection.

Members of the Bloods gang flash their sign.

Many young people turn to gangs due to an unstable family environment. For these teens, the gang appears to serve as a surrogate family. One study of youths in Seattle, Washington, found that teens from one-parent households were 2.4 times as likely to join a gang as other teens. If other adults were present in the home (that is, adults other than the teen's parents), the likelihood of joining a gang increased to three times that of other teens. This research is supported by the statements of many gang members themselves. For example, Joe Jones, a teenage member of the Bloods, a Los Angeles gang, was profiled in the *Los Angeles Times.* He stated, "My dad . . . I don't see him that much. Probably if he was around more, I wouldn't have joined the Bloods. . . . When I first joined, I was lookin' at it like another family." Echoing Jones's statement, Henry, an alias for a twenty-five-year-old gang member quoted by the *Los Angeles Daily News,* said of his fellow gang members: "They are my family. . . . I would die for any of them." As these quotes suggest, the impulse to join a gang is often driven by an attempt to fulfill the need for protection and human connection—needs that are usually provided by one's family.

Community residents march in Trenton, New Jersey, protesting against an increase of gang violence in the city.

An off-duty police officer stands at an L.A. freeway entrance holding a T-shirt emblazoned with a logo calling for an end to gang violence in South Central Los Angeles.

While some young people turn to a gang as an alternative family, others do so in conformity with neighborhood and family traditions of gang membership. For many children in the inner-city neighborhoods of large cities such as Los Angeles and Chicago, gangs are an everyday fact of life. These youths see gang members in the streets and parks, see gang graffiti on the walls, and witness gang violence. Many have family members who are gang members, including older siblings, cousins, uncles, or even mothers and fathers. As these youths approach their teens they begin to experience pressure from friends or family members to join a gang. For many teens these pressures can prove irresistible. According to James C. Howell, a researcher at the National Youth Gang Center, an organization that conducts research on gangs for the federal government, "In some communities, youth are intensively recruited or coerced into gangs. They seemingly have no choice. A few are virtually born into gangs as a result of neighborhood traditions and their parents' earlier (and perhaps continuing) gang participation or involvement in criminal activity." In these circumstances, a young person who resists gang membership is often left isolated from friends and family.

While some youths are essentially forced to join a gang, most choose to do so. In a survey of 1,024 incarcerated gang members conducted by the National Gang Crime Research Center, 73 percent reported that they had volunteered to join their gang. However, many volunteers join not due to the allure of the gang life but in order to escape violence and bullying by neighborhood gangs. As stated by gang expert Steve Nawojczyk, "Many kids are intimidated into gangs to avoid continued harassment. Gangs provide their members and family members with protection from other gangs as well as any other perceived threats." Thus, whether a youth joins a gang due to pressure from family and friends or due to threats by neighborhood gangs, the common factor is the need for inclusion and safety.

As this discussion suggests, while the exact causes of gang membership vary, it is often motivated by a desire for protection and belonging. The motives of gang members are among the issues discussed in *Introducing Issues with Opposing Viewpoints: Gangs,* which includes the following chapters: How Serious Is the Problem of Gangs? What Causes Gang Violence? How Can Gang Violence Be Reduced? These chapters reveal that each individual decision to join a gang has far-reaching and often catastrophic consequences for both gang members and society at large. However, the following pages also show that the gang life is not inevitable. Most young people—including most inner-city youths— are able to steer clear of gang membership and its negative consequences. Christopher, a teenager interviewed by gang author Valerie Wiener, can serve as an inspiration to all who wish to create a life for themselves on their own terms: "I was dependent on myself. I had to take care of my own needs. I played it smart and realized that a gang was trouble. I wanted to live and survive to live life another way."

CHAPTER 1

How Serious Is the Problem of Gangs?

Pueblo Bishops gang members take to the streets of Los Angeles during the Rodney King trial in 1993.

The Problem of Gangs Is Serious

Fight Crime: Invest in Kids

"The sharp increase in youth-gang related homicides is . . . [an] especially ominous trend."

Fight Crime: Invest in Kids is a nonprofit organization that develops new ways to fight crime. Its members include police chiefs, sheriffs, prosecutors, and victims of violence. The following viewpoint is taken from a report written and published by this organization. The authors report that gang violence has increased in recent years. Half of all murders in both Los Angeles and Chicago are gang-related. Gangs are also a problem in smaller cities, towns, and rural areas, according to the authors. Fight Crime: Invest in Kids concludes that while gangs have varying degrees of involvement in drugs and violence, all gangs should be a source of concern to police, parents, and community leaders.

AS YOU READ, CONSIDER THE FOLLOWING QUESTIONS:

1. According to the graph on page nineteen, what percentage of suburban and rural counties has gangs?
2. What are the three types of gangs described by the authors, and how do they differ?
3. How does the membership of the newest form of gangs differ from the previous forms, as described by Fight Crime: Invest in Kids?

Youth-gang related homicides have risen by more than 50 percent according to Professor James Alan Fox, a leading criminologist at Northeastern University. Gang homicides have climbed from 692 in 1999 to over 1,100 in 2002, the latest year for which data is available. Gang-related homicides account for approximately half of all homicides in Chicago, the city that had the highest total number of homicides of any city in the country in 2003. Gang-related homicides also account for approximately half of all homicides in Los Angeles, which led the nation in total homicides the year before (2002).

Gangs are also responsible for the lion's share of juvenile delinquency in smaller cities. A study of troubled youth in Rochester, New York showed that gang members accounted for 68 percent of all the violent acts of delinquency among the youths studied in that city. In Denver, a similar study showed that gang members were responsible for 79 percent of the serious violence committed by that city's youths.

The Spread of Gangs

Los Angeles and Chicago have long been infamous for their traditional gangs: the Crips and Bloods in LA and the Black Gangster Disciples, Latin Kings and Vice Lords in Chicago. But gangs are spreading rapidly throughout the country. According to criminologist Terrence Thomberry, "in the space of about 10 years, gangs have spread from a relatively small number of cities to being a regular feature of the urban landscape." The latest Department of Justice funded National Youth Gang Survey in 2002 confirms that all large cities with populations over 250,000 report having gang activity, as do 87 percent of cities with between 100,000 and 250,000 people. However, gangs are not just in cities: 38 percent of suburban counties and 12 percent of rural counties report gang activity as well.

Former Commander Wayne Wiberg of Chicago's narcotics unit explained that gang members are now appearing in smaller cities and

> **FAST FACT**
>
> Most people think of gangs as groups of boys and young men, but studies have found that in some areas more than one-third of youth gang members are female.

towns throughout Illinois. These towns have "not just people living there who are using drugs, but people living there that are selling."

The Development and Types of Gangs
Youth gangs have been around for a long time. In the early 19th century, youth gangs were primarily Irish, Jewish, and Italian when many members of those immigrant groups lived in economically deprived neighborhoods and endured ethnic or religious discrimination. According to the most recent National Youth Gang Survey, nearly half of all gang members are Hispanic and a third are African American. The most recent gangs forming in smaller cities and suburbs in the 1990s, however, are more likely to be mixed ethnically, and involve female, white, and middle-class youths. Gangs vary tremendously, but it is helpful to think in terms of three different categories: traditional gangs; more recent crews, cliques, or posses; and gangs forming in smaller cities, rural areas, and suburbs during the 1990s.

Traditional Gangs
The gangs forming before the mid-1980s tended to fit the traditional definition of gangs. They began defending turf but often evolved into very large organizations that became more involved in drug sales and other criminal activity. Automatic weapons and drive-by shootings replaced the fists, chains and knives used in earlier gang violence. While the average size of traditional gangs is about 180 members, a few of these gangs number in the thousands and even tens of thousands and have formed very elaborate structures and rules similar in many ways to the Mafia. Some gangs, such as the Crips and the Bloods from Los Angeles attempted to set up chapters in other cities. However, most expansion of gangs was homegrown or due to members simply moving to other cities, rather than a more concerted franchising effort.

More Recent Crews, Cliques, or Posses
Many cities, like Washington, D.C., and Philadelphia, have relatively few of the larger, more traditional gangs, and instead have more loosely structured neighborhood "crews," "cliques," or "posses." These small drug or neighborhood gangs often number only 25 members, and there is less gang graffiti, hand signs, and "colors" associated with these groups. Still, "Live by the neighborhood, die by the neighborhood"

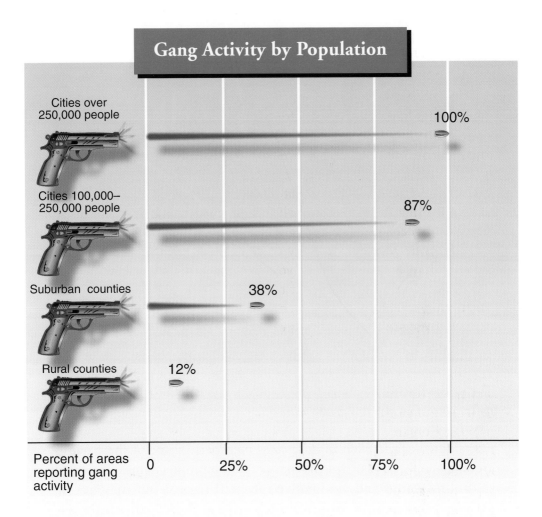

Gang Activity by Population

Cities over
250,000 people
100%

Cities 100,000–
250,000 people
87%

Suburban counties
38%

Rural counties
12%

Percent of areas
reporting gang
activity

0   25%   50%   75%   100%

Source: National Youth Gang Center, 2002.

is a common sentiment for these smaller gangs. These neighborhood gangs that often formed during the early 1980s are the most likely of any of the three categories of gangs to be involved in drug sales.

Gangs Forming in Smaller Cities, Rural Areas, and the Suburbs During the 1990s

Compared to the more traditional gangs and the crews, cliques, or posses that formed in the 1980s, the newer gangs forming in smaller cities, rural areas, and the suburbs beginning in the 1990s tend to be less involved in both drug sales and violence. As mentioned above, these newer gangs are often more diverse, and more likely to have

Members of the Crips in Los Angeles pose with their weapons. Although traditional gangs confined their organization to a single city, the Crips, a gang that formed in Los Angeles in the late 1960s, tried to expand to other cities.

white, female, and even middle-class members. Some of these gangs are small collections of youths that take on ominous names similar to traditional gangs and are involved in graffiti, etc., but may not be especially violent or heavily involved in drug sales. Nevertheless the difference between some of these newer gangs and other earlier gangs may not be that great, and parents, the police, and communities need to be vigilant. These newer gangs may become more dangerous over time. There are also very violent inner-city drug gangs or more traditional-style gangs, such as the El Salvadoran dominated MS-13, whose members are moving into the older, close-in suburbs near many cities.

An Ominous Trend

From a peak in the early 1990s, violent crime and homicide rates have dropped dramatically. But there is no room for Americans to become complacent. Violent crime in America is still at unacceptable levels: in 2001 over 16,000 Americans lost their lives to violence. And in 2002, homicides were up over two percent and then again another one percent for the first six months of 2003 (the latest available national figures). When crime last began to spike upwards in the late 1980s and early 1990s cities with more than one million people were the first cities to see crime go up and then the first to see it come down. So it is alarming that homicides were heading up almost six percent in those largest cities for the first six months of 2003. And certainly the sharp increase in youth-gang related homicides is a related and especially ominous trend.

Crime costs Americans $655 billion a year. Most of that cost is borne by the millions of victims, but Americans also pay $90 billion a year in taxes for criminal justice system expenses and an additional $65 billion a year in total private security costs. The taxes and private security payments alone average $535 a year for every man, woman and child in America. That is over $2,000 for a family of four even if no one in that family becomes a victim of the more than 23 million crimes committed each year in the United States. In a 1998 study, Professor Mark A. Cohen of

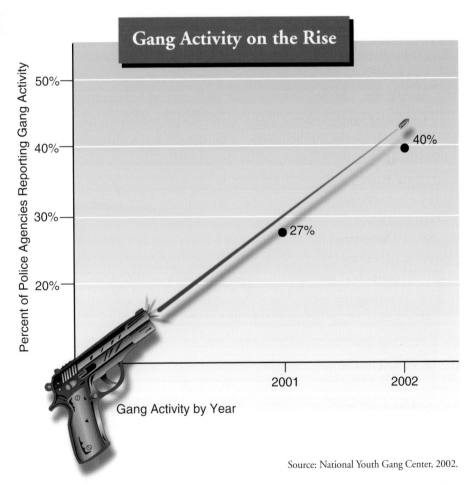

Source: National Youth Gang Center, 2002.

Vanderbilt University looked at the cost issue from another perspective. He found that preventing one teen from adopting a life of crime would save the country between $1.7 million and $2.3 million. The Department of Justice reports that "if the 2001 rates of incarceration were to continue indefinitely" a white male in the United States would have a 1 in 17 chance of going to state or federal prison during his lifetime, a Hispanic male would have a 1 in 6 chance and a black male would have a 1 in 3 chance of going to prison. However one looks at it—the more than 16,000 homicides a year, the millions of young men and women who will be imprisoned, or the shattered lives of the survivors of crime—crime and violence continue to challenge the very soul of America.

Real Hope for Reducing the Toll of Gang Violence

After years of contentious debate about whether to be tougher or more compassionate with criminals, a consensus is beginning to emerge in some communities. The consensus is based on a combination of research, hard experience gained from those in closest contact with these troubled youths, and a willingness by policy-makers to leave ideological suppositions behind to adopt tested, proven solutions. Law enforcement leaders are often leading this change. The real solutions are to be found in becoming smarter about crime, which requires new policies that are both tough and compassionate. If the right policies are followed, the huge costs and the lives lost because of violent crime can be sharply reduced.

EVALUATING THE AUTHORS' USE OF STATISTICS:

In the viewpoint you just read, the authors cited statistics to argue that the problem of gang violence is increasing. The authors of the next viewpoint use statistics to argue that media coverage of gang violence has increased even though gang violence itself has not. Which author uses statistics more persuasively? After reading both viewpoints, do you believe the rise in gang violence is real or media exaggeration?

VIEWPOINT 2

The Problem of Gangs Is Exaggerated by the Media

Richard C. McCorkle and Terance D. Miethe

"The media's coverage of gangs is distorted."

In the following viewpoint Richard C. McCorkle and Terance D. Miethe argue that the problem of gangs is not as serious as the news media have led the public to believe. They insist that the number of news stories involving gangs has increased dramatically even though there is no evidence that the gang problem itself has grown. Besides overreporting the problem, McCorkle and Miethe continue, the media also use sensationalist language when presenting stories about gangs. For example, they describe gangs as "hoodlum bands" and "urban terrorists." This language further exaggerates the problem and leads to unnecessary fear among news readers and viewers.

Richard C. McCorkle is an associate professor of criminal justice at the University of Nevada, Las Vegas. Terance D. Miethe is a professor of criminal justice at the University of Nevada, Las Vegas. He is the author of several books, including *Crime and Its Social Context* and *Rethinking Homicide*. McCorkle and Miethe are coauthors of *Panic: The Social Construction of the Street Gang Problem,* from which the following viewpoint was taken.

AS YOU READ, CONSIDER THE FOLLOWING QUESTIONS:
1. By what percentage did the coverage of gangs by the *Honolulu Star Bulletin* increase, as reported by McCorkle and Miethe?
2. According to the authors, what types of crimes are gang members most likely to be charged with?
3. According to McCorkle and Miethe, how do the police influence media coverage of the gang problem?

The public's primary source of information about gangs, and a major actor in the gang phenomenon itself, is the media. Coverage of gangs has exploded during recent years. A search of major U.S. newspapers and magazines from 1983 to 1999 reveals that media coverage of gangs increased by nearly 2500 percent.

While the extent to which this kind of national coverage accurately reflected an increased gang threat cannot be determined, the findings from a study of gang news in Hawaii raise serious doubts. Paul Perrone and Meda Chesney-Lind conducted a content analysis [a review of what topics were covered] of the *Honolulu Star Bulletin* for 1987 through 1996. While there was no evidence of a dramatic increase in gang membership or gang activity, over those 10 years the coverage of gangs in the newspaper increased by 4000 percent! . . .

Distorted Media Coverage

The media's coverage of gangs is distorted in a number of ways. Little accurate or useful information is thus actually provided to the public about the extent and nature of the gang problem in this country. Noted gang researcher Walter Miller opines:

A prime source of misconception about gangs is the mass media. Almost everyone except those whose professional activities bring them in direct and continuing contact with gangs depends on information from media coverage. What the media choose to report about gangs, the kinds of gangs they select for attention, and even whether they choose to report on gangs at all, are determined by considerations only indirectly related to the actual situation. Most of what the average observer "knows" about gangs stems from a series of editorial decisions oriented primarily to the question "What is newsworthy?" rather than "What is accurate?"

One popular misconception comes from media reports linking the growth of gangs to the migration of big-city gangs to mid-size and small cities. Such a conclusion is not supported by the research: Most gangs emerge from indigenous groupings within communities. Neither do gangs, as the media frequently reports, dominate crack cocaine markets. Gang members do sell crack, and other drugs as well, but use is far more common than sales and even involvement in sales is low.

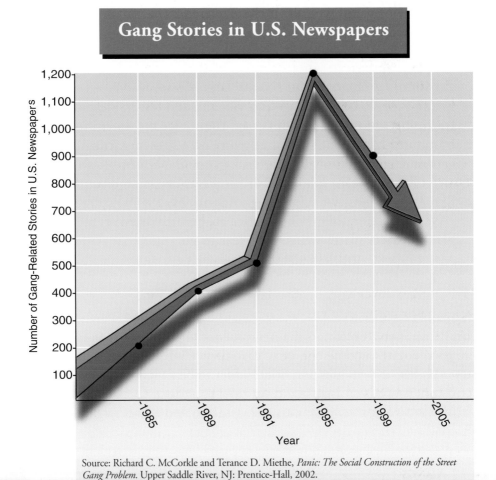

Gang Stories in U.S. Newspapers

Source: Richard C. McCorkle and Terance D. Miethe, *Panic: The Social Construction of the Street Gang Problem.* Upper Saddle River, NJ: Prentice-Hall, 2002.

Perhaps the greatest distortion concerns gang violence. Gang scholar Malcolm Klein examined newspaper coverage of street gangs in Los Angeles and found that most stories focused on violent offenses: shootings, stabbings, and beatings. Arrest statistics, however, indicated that gang members were far more likely to be charged with property crimes, drug offenses, and truancy.

Critical of his own newspaper's focus on gang violence, *Los Angeles Times* reporter David Freed notes that in 1991 the paper carried 411 gang shootings involving 615 victims; incidents involving another 8,000 crime victims received no mention in the press. John Hagedorn similarly found little correspondence between the *Milwaukee Sentinel's* coverage of local gangs and his own in-depth research of gangs and gang activity in that city.

Sensationalized Stories

Like crime stories generally, media reports of gang crime are highly inflammatory and sensationalized. Stories on even minor confrontations involving gangs typically include references to "urban terrorism," "war," "hoodlum bands," and "gang war battles."

> If many American ghettos now resemble Beirut [a city in Lebanon], *urban terrorists* . . . are largely responsible, acting as roving gangs peddling drugs and violence and terror. Despite the fratricide among gangs, most of their victims are innocent bystanders. . . . Hungry for customers, a growing number of gangs are going national, with black gangs like Los Angeles' Crips and Chicago's Disciples establishing franchises in cities from Seattle to Shreveport. (*LA Times,* August 24, 1987)
>
> Whole sections of urban America are being written off as *anarchic badlands,* places where cops fear to go. . . . (*U.S. News and World Report,* April 10, 1980)

Spreading Fear

In the war between gangs, the news media suggest no one is safe, that anyone could become the next casualty. One national newspaper reports that "everyone is potential fodder to be a victim." Naive media consumers are even instructed on how to reduce their risks of confrontation with a *gangsta* with a fragile ego and a hair trigger.

Police arrest a gang member suspected of dealing drugs. Some experts argue that the media exaggerate gang involvement in the drug trade.

Keep your eyes to yourself. Read your paperback. Read your magazine. Do not make eye contact. They are children so wary of any "dis" they might "smoke" you for staring. (*Mother Jones,* January–February 1994)

Metaphors are used frequently depicting gangs as a "terminal disease" and the tone of reporting generally encourages a fatalistic attitude toward the gang problem.

Gangs are growing like a cancer. (*U.S. News and World Report,* April 8, 1991)

The time has come to talk of gangstas. Actually, the time is long past. We should've talked of gangstas 10 or 15 years ago when

Southern California killers made mass murder a drive-through convenience. Should've broached the discussion when the boys in the 'hood started turning on one another with savage ferocity and the graveyards began to fill with children not yet old enough to shave. . . . But we didn't speak up . . . and now here we sit, in the grip of gangstas. . . . (*Miami Herald,* September 19, 1993)

Modern gangs are well organized, and most of their members are more concerned with being ostracized than with the eventuality of bleeding to death on the street. . . . If there are solutions to the gang plague, they will not be easy to effect. (*Arizona Republic,* April 18, 1993) . . .

Relying on Police for Crime Information

How can we account for the manner in which the media cover crime and gangs? . . . [A] convincing explanation for the media's coverage of crime points to the process through which crime stories are collected and the criteria used to determine newsworthiness. Each day the media are confronted with a large number of potential crime stories, simply because (nonviolent) crime is consistently available and abundant. To make the production of crime news more manageable, the media routinize the task by placing themselves in positions where there is *easy access to credible crime news stories.* . . .

Journalists limit their news-gathering to press releases and interview quotations from source organizations, primarily the police. By relying on police, crime news becomes easy news and also offers journalists protections from claims of bias. In every city across the country, police supply news organizations with a steady stream of crime incidents ("crime blotters"). In smaller towns, information regarding all crimes may be supplied; in large urban areas, police usually provide only a summary of a subset of crime events. Moreover, most cities have full-time reporters at police stations and are frequently provided with the written reports of crimes submitted by investigative officers. . . .

Due to the dependence of the news media, the police are allowed to shape public images of crime and crime control. Reporters simply serve as conduits for police views of crime while at the same time presenting their reports as unbiased. . . . By simply rewriting police releases as crime news items, by failing to think critically about the processes and events observed and by failing to ask pertinent questions, the police become the primary definers of crime and crime control to the public.

Shaping Public Perceptions of the Gang Problem

Findings from two studies suggest that the media shape the public's perception of the gang problem. In a survey of residents in a small city in Wisconsin, Susan Takata and Richard Zevitz found that adults were more likely than youth to describe the threat of gangs as "very serious," a pattern ascribed to the fact that adults were more likely to have relied on news reporting for their information about gangs in the city.

A second survey of adults in Indianapolis by Douglas Pryor and Edmund McGarrell more clearly demonstrates the impact of the media on assessments of the gang problem. While most survey respondents did not view gangs as a serious problem in their neighborhood, those

Police officers question a member of the L.A. Crips.

who had watched a gang story on a television newscast were more likely to perceive gangs as "quite" serious in other parts of the city. Pryor and McGarrell concluded:

> For most individuals, youth gang crime is seen as a serious, escalating, and dangerous problem, but one that is a problem "over there"—that is, in other parts of the city. We suggest that this reflects the tendency for perceptions of youth gang crime in "other areas" to be shaped by stereotypes and media presentations. . . .

Police Manipulation of the Media

Crime stories are a staple of news reporting, but the image of crime and gangs presented by the media is grossly distorted. This distortion is due, in part, by media judgments regarding what is newsworthy—in short, what will sell. Distorted images of crime and gangs also are the result of the media's reliance on the police for information. Enjoying a near-monopoly on crime information, police officials supply the media accounts of crime and police practices that place law enforcement in a favorable light and further organizational interests.

It seems reasonable to conclude that the police have utilized the media to promote their claims regarding street gangs. By presenting police accounts of gang activity as objective and unbiased, the media fosters a distorted image of gangs in the mind of the public. By manipulating the media, the police are also able to increase organizational resources and powers.

EVALUATING THE AUTHORS' USE OF QUOTES:

In the viewpoint you just read, the authors rely extensively on quotes from newspapers and newsmagazines to support their view that the media overstate the gang problem. Does this use of quotes increase the effectiveness of the authors' arguments? Why or why not?

Gangs Are a Problem in Rural Areas

Mark Sappenfield

"Rural America has a gang problem."

Gangs have traditionally been viewed as an inner-city phenomenon. However, in recent years, many experts have warned of an increase of gangs in small towns, suburbs, and rural areas. In the following viewpoint, Mark Sappenfield, a staff writer for the *Christian Science Monitor,* reports that gangs have indeed spread to rural places. In the process, they have brought gang-style violence and drug selling to areas that were once considered immune from such influences.

AS YOU READ, CONSIDER THE FOLLOWING QUESTIONS:

1. According to the U.S. Department of Justice study cited by the author, what percentage of cities with populations between 1,000 and 2,500 had gangs arrive between 1970 and 1998?
2. What are three causes of the rise of gangs in rural America cited by Sappenfield?

Glenn County [California] is hardly a place that conjures up images of gang violence. This is a land scratched from the tender Sacramento Valley earth in endless rows of almond trees, nodding fields of wheat, and plains as flat and hot as a baking sheet.

Along Interstate 5 north, it is a rest stop on the way to no place in particular. In an area larger than Rhode Island, there are seven stoplights.

Yet it is here, in this isolated agricultural cradle, that someone stopping for gas was chased and stabbed for wearing rival gang colors. It is here that a teen was killed in a shooting at the local cinema.

The stories are the same across the iron belt of upper Minnesota, the cornfields of Illinois, and the alpine valleys of Utah. Rural America has a gang problem.

Into the Heartland

What began a decade ago with the widening of the drug trade and the migration of many gang members has now taken root in the heartland. Searching for a sense of belonging and the trappings of a seemingly more exciting urban life, farm workers' sons and high-school dropouts have swelled the ranks of rural gangs, bringing street fights and shootings to areas that had only seen such things on [the television crime show] "NYPD Blue."

While gangs remain a more pressing problem in cities, their spread into even the most remote niches of America has upended the small-town idyll of communities nationwide. As a result, these towns are transforming their law-enforcement efforts, seeing gangs as a primary public-safety concern.

"There has been much more activity in rural areas . . . in the past 10 years," says Walter Miller, a consultant to the US Department of Justice in Cambridge, Mass.

He himself documented the trend in one study for the Justice Department that traced youth gangs from 1970 to 1998. Most notably, 41 percent more cities with populations between 1,000 to 2,500 people saw gangs arrive by 1998.

Expanding the Drug Trade

The reasons for the jump vary from region to region. In Midwestern towns, law-enforcement officials say gangs in Chicago and Minneapolis have spread their crack-cocaine trade farther beyond beltways. "Its all price driven," says Jim Wright of the Minnesota Gang Strike Force in Duluth. "If you can drive five or six hours and make five times more money, you're going to do it."

The last two murders there have been gang-related, and when a gang member went on trial across the border in Wisconsin 1-1/2 years ago, the prosecutor's house was firebombed. In Mount Vernon, Ill., at the height of its gang problem in 1994, the community of 17,000 had six homicides.

A member of the Sureño gang shows off his tattooed knuckles. In recent years, evidence suggests that the gang problem has spread from America's cities into rural areas.

Yet in many parts of the West, gangs seem to have flourished for a different reason: boredom. Here in Glenn County, where a trip to the big city means driving to Chico, gangs offer something to do—an escape from the agricultural depression that grips the county.

A Typical Pattern

Authorities first started seeing gang graffiti in the early 1990s. Since then, a dozen gangs have sprouted among the 27,000 residents. Most

Gang graffiti covers an abandoned train station in rural Virginia. In the early 1990s, gang graffiti began appearing in a number of rural areas throughout the United States.

are overwhelmingly Hispanic, and for these youths, the county is divided as clearly as Belfast [a city in Northern Ireland]. Orland and Hamilton City are split between the Sureños and the Norteños—two Mexican gangs born in San Quentin prison in 1968. According to legend, a member of the Sureños moved to Orland, and a Hamilton City resident returned from prison as a Norteño, beginning the rivalry.

It's a typical pattern, says Joan Liquin of the Logan-Cache County Gang Project in Utah. Migration of gang members—either voluntarily or through juvenile-relocation programs—has spurred the growth of gangs in her area. In four years, the number of gang members there has risen from 45 to 330. As in Glenn County, most gang-related crimes have been minor: Thefts, vandalism, and fistfights top the list.

Dropping Out

These are charges that Francisco knows well. But the teen hardly seems like a gang-banger. For one, he smiles too much. In fact, he's good-natured and laughing, even when talking about run-ins with the police as a member of the Sureños.

FAST FACT

The migration of gangs from the city to the country is usually not the result of a gang's attempt to expand criminal enterprises. Rather, it is the result of individual gang members' relocation due to personal and family-related reasons.

He talks in past tense, though, because—with the help of Glenn County's Project Exito—he has dropped out.

"I just got tired of always getting in trouble," says Francisco (not his real name). "Half the guys I used to hang out with don't like me anymore. . . . But last time I got out of juvenile hall, I got tired of being there."

Standing nearby, Sal Hernandez and Ulises Tellechea long to hear these words more often. While the federally funded program brings together all sorts of people—from teachers to probation officers—to help at-risk teens, Messrs. Hernandez and Tellechea have the task of befriending as many gang members as possible. . . .

There are setbacks, Tellechea says, like when a teen he's working with ends up back in juvenile hall—not to mention the fact that Orland

and Hamilton City kids still won't do anything together. But many signs are positive, both here and nationwide.

National statistics suggest that rural gang activity peaked in the mid-1990s and is gradually declining. In Glenn County, law-enforcement officials see less graffiti and violence. The stabbing and shooting happened more than a year ago.

And Tellechea is also seeing a difference. "One of the kids asked me to go shopping because he didn't want to wear his gang clothes anymore," he says. "He said, 'I want to dress like you.'"

EVALUATING THE AUTHORS' ARGUMENTS:

The viewpoint you just read is a newspaper report on the spread of gangs to rural areas. The next viewpoint, by Mike Males, takes a critical look at a similar journalist account from the *Los Angeles Times* of the spread of gangs to suburban Orange County. After reading both viewpoints, consider whether any of Males's criticisms of the *Los Angeles Times* story apply to Sappenfield's article. For example, does Sappenfield supply convincing statistics to back up his claim that gang violence has increased significantly in rural areas? Or does he rely more on anecdotal evidence? Does Sappenfield use language that creates a sense of alarm? Or is his writing style generally straightforward?

Gangs Are Not a Problem in the Suburbs

Mike Males

"It's hard to imagine how white suburban kids . . . could be acting any better."

Mike Males is a sociology instructor at the University of California, Santa Cruz, and a senior researcher at the Center on Juvenile and Criminal Justice, an organization that conducts research on the justice system. He frequently writes on youth issues for various publications. The following viewpoint is taken from his book *Kids and Guns: How Politicians, Experts, and the Press Fabricate Fear of Youth.* In it Males rejects the idea that gangs are spreading to rural and suburban areas. Specifically, he responds to a *Los Angeles Times* article claiming that gangs are invading the wealthy suburbs of Orange County, California. Males contends there is no factual basis for this purported trend. The storied rise of suburban gangs is a fabrication invented by the media and politicians, he concludes.

AS YOU READ, CONSIDER THE FOLLOWING QUESTIONS:
1. How did rates of urban gang violence change in the late 1990s, as reported by Males?
2. How many Orange County youths were arrested for murder in the 1990s, according to the author?
3. As stated by Males, how did television news coverage of murder change between 1992 and 1996?

Mike Males, *Kids and Guns: How Politicians, Experts, and the Press Fabricate Fear of Youth.* Monroe, ME: Common Courage Press, 2000. Copyright © 2000 by Mike Males. Reproduced by permission.

In 1999, as prison, law enforcement, political, academic, and news media interests grappled with schemes to keep the public frightened in an era of plummeting crime, there appeared on the front page of America's largest urban daily the most dangerously silly story on youth I saw in a decade of press excess. "GANGS," breathed the *Los Angeles Times'* April 18, 1999, cover feature, had invaded the "south Orange County haven."

The law-and-order lobby [people who advocate strict laws against crime] faced a formidable problem. In the late 1990s, real urban gang violence had plunged. From their early-decade peaks, murder rates among Los Angeles's black, Hispanic, and Asian youths fell by 85%, reaching three-decade lows by 1999. They would decline another 13% in 2000. Had he not been murdered in 1996, gangsta-emeritus [retired gang member] Tupac Shakur would have composed very different rhymes about a Los Angeles of 1999 and 2000, where only one black youth per month was arrested for murder—down from one every 80 hours in 1990. Fewer mobile-cam homicide scenes appeared on evening news. The increasingly detached larger public and its fickle news media lost interest in far-away inner city problems.

As fears waned that mobs of ghetto "superpredators" would pillage pristine suburbs, the *Times,* along with other major media and authorities, cranked up a relentless crusade to convince suburban folks that they now were in dire peril from their *own* murderous, drugged-out kids. The new fear agenda declared that every downtown evil now menaced tract-home paradise—only its agents were no longer downtown kids, but paradise's own pampered spawn. And things would only get worse. As "chilling" (the press's workhorse adjective) as the ubiquitous youth menace was now, police chief after politician after expert intoned to the cameras and in print, it would all get worse, because the teenage population was *growing*.

The Creation of a Fictional Killer

Hence, the creation of the suburban teen killer. And what better setting than South Orange County, California, one of the whitest, most conservative, largest areas of concentrated wealth in the Milky Way? . . .

Now, "the specter of gangs" had invaded the richest right-wing citadel, the *Times* reported in Scream 3 tone. Reporter Bonnie Harris's elephantine story exhaled "gang" dozens of times. Now, truly, no place is safe. The folks in Orange County's posh "suburban refuge," the "sanctuary" where "crime is so rare" that "there have been just three killings in 10 years," couldn't comprehend the terror unleashed on their "clean, safe, kid-friendly streets" by . . . "*gangs,*" Harris declared.

Not a Real Gang

What chicanery. It turned out that was three more murders than anyone blamed on South Hills gangs. Harris's story cited no Richie Rich G-ridin', unless you count a couple of "minor scrapes" by five James-Dean retro teens who called themselves the "Slick 50's" and dressed like "Jim Stark, teenager from a good family" (in Warner Bros. famous *Rebel* poster from 1954). But wait—several Slick 50's were present

A newspaper headline sensationalizes the public's fear that gangs are invading suburban America.

"Not in My Neighborhood!"
Teen Gangs Invade the Suburbs

Norman Booth was worried about his son. When William was in his early teens, the tall, lean track star became mesmerized with gang culture, primarily from gangster rap videos he watched on TV. Before long, William emulated it. "He'd only wear certain colors, and his baseball cap was always turned the same way," recalls his father, who always insisted his son change his attire.

Adopted at the age of 7 by Norman and Nancy Booth, William had come from a lifetime of abuse. Yet, amid the rolling farmlands of Zumbrota, Minnesota, he grew into a young man who played lovingly with his siblings. Then in 1993, the couple divorced, and William went to live with his mother. Three years later William returned to his dad's house for his sophomore year. "His grades were poor, but he excelled at track," remembers Booth, who enjoyed training with his son.

But William wanted something faster. When he turned 18, he moved to Grand Rapids, Minnesota—a town of just 8,400 residents—and was soon hanging out with one of the town's three gangs. Booth's attempts to contact and dissuade his son were to no avail, so, distraught, he went to the police. "William's gang was known to the officers, but its crimes were considered minor—mostly theft and vandalism," says Norman, who felt reassured.

Two days later, on October 29, 1997, a sheriff's deputy informed Booth that his son had been brutally murdered with a shotgun and knife. The teen's body had been found near an abandoned mine outside of Grand Rapids.

At press time, seven of the eight indicted in the slaying of William Booth had pleaded guilty to various second-degree murder charges in exchange for lighter sentencing or testimony. (Due to a prior hung jury, the eighth gang member will be tried again later this month.) Though Norman isn't sure why William was killed, he heard it was because he'd lost his "colors" (the blue-and-white bandanna that gang members wear on their left bicep or hanging from their left-back pocket to show unity), which was a punishable offense.

when a stabbing occurred outside a party 10 months earlier, back in summer 1998. The victim had long since recovered. The attacker, a 21-year-old, was not a "Slick." . . .

Details. Four "Slick 50's," denying gangstaship, politely posed on a verdant hilltop for the story's cover picture. Precisely the point: if these sweetly grinning whiteboys straight outa suburbia wore matching red-white jackets and called each other the special home-names, it was just a matter of time before the Ridgeline Parkway Crips and Pacific Coast Highway Bloods commenced to blastin' Fashion Island [shopping mall] and the Newport Yacht Harbor with the nine-mill'er. This was the crazed evil-kid proliferation logic dispensed by the press and the experts it quoted: if one or two of them can be, all of them can be, and if all of them can be, all of them are.

Sowing Fear

Not even the most compelling facts could dent the scare propaganda. Down these mean equestrian trails of Orange County's upscale burgs . . . where half a million people dwell, ONE youth was arrested for murder during the entire decade—back in 1993. Nor were things getting worse; far from it. In 1979, 15 white youths . . . were arrested for homicide. No year since even approached half that peak. In fact, 1997, 1998, 1999, and 2000 (two, zero, zero, and zero white-kid murder arrests, respectively) represented decades-long lows. Back in the 1970s, 5,000 Orange County white kids were popped for felonies every year. In 2000, 1,310. Short of perfection, it's hard to imagine how white suburban kids—and, against much steeper socioeconomic odds, black, Latino, and Asian youths as well—could be acting any better.

No matter. . . . The 1999 press and big institutions lusted for young blood.

The more crime plummeted—Orange County's rate fell a staggering 44% for violent offenses and 63% for property offenses from 1990 to 2000—the more frantically feverish the police and press fear campaign became. A national study by the Center on Media and Public Affairs found that as homicide rates fell 20% from 1992 to 1996, coverage of murder stories on ABC, CBS, and NBC news rose sevenfold. In Southern California as elsewhere, the smallest youth transgression ballooned into an "alarming new crisis" accentuated with inflamed "expert" commentary. "Hundreds" of "gun incidents" in

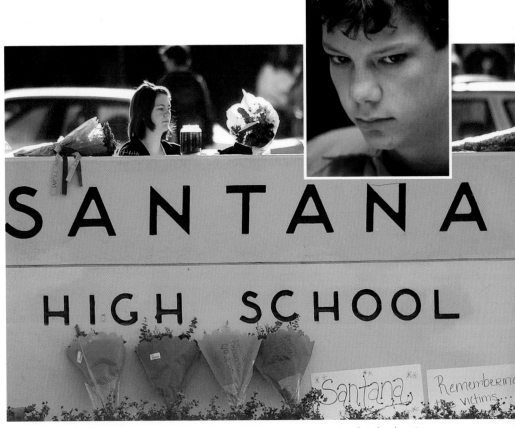

In 2001 Andy Williams (inset) went on a shooting spree at Santana High School in Santee, California, that left two students dead and thirteen others seriously injured.

Orange County schools! (Nearly all involved BBs or cap pistols). "Disturbing" Fullerton High School student cheating! "Alarming" vandalism by four teens! Drugged-out teenage wastoids wrecking the peace of pastoral mountain-town Ojai (where, the story failed to mention, an enraged 44-year-old recently chased his wife and three kids down a lane, gunning down each and then himself). The toll from the *Times'* barrage of page-one youth-gone-wild megafeatures, including the south county "gang" scourge: 0 dead, 1 injury, heavy casualties to rural mailboxes.

But don't be fooled, press alarmists hinted: the very *lack* of visible crime meant there must be a huge, subterranean, therefore *even scarier* youth barbarity lurking under the tranquil surface. After all, quiet Littleton, Colorado; Springfield, Oregon; Jonesboro, Arkansas; Santee, California, were blindsided by towhead school shooters packing heavy steel. Capitalizing on the new fear, books stuffing psychology shelves in job lots pronounced suburban teens a "generation in crisis," "a tribe apart," an "anticultural" mob perpetrating unheard-of savageries in knotty-pined rec rooms, heroin lanes, and parents' king-sized beds. That this suburban youth-crisis epidemic showed up nowhere in morgue, hospital, drug, murder, school dropout, crime, pregnancy, AIDS, school testing, TV-gazing, or any other standard index of trouble cooled no flaming jets. In the 1990s, it became acceptable to expand the rarest teenage anecdote into an emblem of mass generational wastage, to manufacture statistics and recycle them endlessly until no one knew where they originated, to just make things up.

EVALUATING THE AUTHOR'S ARGUMENTS:

In the viewpoint you just read, the author adopts a satirical writing style in order to emphasize what he views as the absurdity of the media's claim that gangs are spreading into the suburbs. Identify two examples of the author's use of sarcasm. Does this technique make the author's argument more or less compelling? Why?

CHAPTER 2

What Causes Gang Violence?

A member of the Mob Crew gang poses with weapons in Los Angeles.

A Lack of Morality Is the Cause of Gang Violence

"[Gang members] live in a moral vacuum that gives them no sense of right and wrong and has no place for compassion, respect or responsibility."

Richard Williamson

Gang experts cite various reasons why young people join gangs and engage in violence, drug dealing, and other crimes. In the following selection, journalist Richard Williamson argues that the main cause of such behavior is an absence of moral values among the youths who join gangs. Writing about the gang problem in Birmingham, England, Williamson maintains that gangsters in that city have created a separate, parallel culture of lawlessness, violence, and disregard for the societal norms that the majority of citizens live by. Prior to his death in December 2003, Richard Williamson was a feature writer and columnist for the *Sunday Mercury,* a weekly newspaper in Birmingham, England.

AS YOU READ, CONSIDER THE FOLLOWING QUESTIONS:

1. Why are today's gang members more frightening than the traditional Mafia, according to Williamson?
2. What must the black and Asian communities do in response to the gang problem, according to the author?
3. In the author's opinion, why is it important to create a tolerant, inclusive society?

G

un-toting gangsters shooting a rival in a barber's shop is a scene straight from a Mafia movie. [1]

Except that this was the work of the gangs of Birmingham [England], not New York.

The young thugs running wild on our streets may live in a Hollywood-inspired fantasy but the bullets are real and the victims don't get up and walk away when the shooting is over.

These black and Asian gangs may be no more than a crude parody of the real Mafia but in one sense they are even more frightening.

Traditional mafiosi may have been driven by evil but they still craved a connection with the legitimate world, often aspiring to the lifestyle of the wealthy middle-class.

Our gangs are completely different.

Soulless Killers

These are volatile, rootless young men who reject the world in which the rest of us live. They are violent and ruthless, place no value on human life and lack any sense of morality.

Behind the flash cars, sharp clothes and bundles of cash lurk soulless killers with no stake in society.

Offering rewards for their capture merely plays to the shallow vanity of self-styled outlaws who will see a price on their heads as a mark of status.

Armed police on the streets may be comforting to law-abiding citizens but they won't deter boys with guns anxious to live up to the myth they have created for themselves.

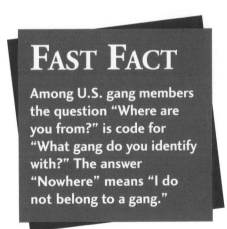

FAST FACT

Among U.S. gang members the question "Where are you from?" is code for "What gang do you identify with?" The answer "Nowhere" means "I do not belong to a gang."

The fact that they are fantasists makes them more, rather than less, dangerous.

---

1. On January 2, 2003, teenagers Letisha Shakespeare and Charlene Ellis were shot dead outside a party at a Birmingham, England, hair salon.

A police officer searches a youth in London. A rise in crime has led to increased police activity in that city.

. . . The mothers of slain teenagers Letisha Shakespeare and Charlene Ellis warned of the terror inflicted on the street and the fear that shuts the mouths of witnesses.

A Complex Issue

We should not under-estimate the power of the gangs but the biggest mistake we can make now is to assume that the issues are simple.

Of course, the best outcome would be to sweep the scum off the streets and lock them up for good—but will that stop the next generation of disaffected youths from taking their place?

What we must do is understand how this appalling situation developed in the first place before we can make any progress to a lasting solution.

Sadly, some people will say: 'They are bad because they are black.'

That is not only irrational and grossly insulting to the decent majority but also likely to make a bad situation worse.

A gang member flashes his gang sign over his face after he is arrested.

SURVIVED THE WORLD AT WAR. SURVIVED KOREA, VIETNAM AND THE PERSIAN GULF.

SURVIVED YEARS OF SCHOOL. SURVIVED DECADES OF A CAREER.

SURVIVED CREATING A HOME AND A FAMILY.

SURVIVED THE CHANGES AND TURMOIL OF THE 20th CENTURY.

SURVIVED DECADES OF MARRIAGE. SURVIVED GRANDKIDS. SURVIVED IT ALL...

IN ORDER TO BE CUT DOWN WITHOUT A SECOND THOUGHT BY SOME ANTISOCIAL KID.

WELL, HE WAS, YOU KNOW, KIND OF IN MY WAY...

BY GREENBERG FOR THE SEATTLE POST-INTELLIGENCER

Source: Greenberg. © 1997 by the *Seattle Post-Intelligencer*. Reproduced by permission.

It is no more acceptable than Asians blaming the 'corrupt' West for leading their sons astray.

Others put it down to turf wars over control of the drugs trade.

Drugs certainly play a major part but it would be naive to think that this is the sole cause of the problems we face.

A criminal underworld needs to finance itself and, just as the Kray twins [brothers who led a London gang in the 1950s and 1960s] turned to extortion and protection rackets, so today's gangsters get their cash from narcotics.

A Parallel Universe

But this is simply the currency of a secret country about which we know little or nothing. These vicious young men go beyond anything we understand as conventional criminality.

They have constructed for themselves a separate culture that rejects all the values that the rest of us live by. They recognise no laws, speak their own language and live by their own warped rules.

Those who criticise the police might want to reflect on the difficulties of breaking into a complex subculture that amounts to a parallel universe.

Neither an iron fist nor throwing millions of quid [British currency] at community projects is going to provide a quick fix.

It is tough and will take courage but the black and Asian communities are going to have to deliver up their renegades to the law. They must do this for the sake of future generations.

The task for all of us is to build a genuinely inclusive society based on tolerance and equality for all, regardless of race, religion or class.

It has to be a world in which education, housing, healthcare and jobs are free of discrimination.

There can be no 'keep out' signs, no 'unwelcome' mats at the door.

We have seen what happens when those who feel rejected and alienated go away to build an anti-society of their own.

Police officers question a suspected gang member in Fresno, California.

It may give them a bogus sense of 'belonging' that they don't find in the world of their parents, neighbours and fellow citizens but they live in a moral vacuum that gives them no sense of right and wrong and has no place for compassion, respect or responsibility.

The worst thing of all is to shrug and say: 'So what? As long as they are only killing each other, why should we care?' That will simply reinforce the sense of two societies—the mainstream one to which 99 per cent of us belong and the small, malign, world of the outlaws.

We must guard against the gangsters gathering to themselves a glamorous allure that will attract impressionable kids who think it really is Gunfight at the OK Corral instead of recognising the grubby reality of violent thuggery that brings nothing but misery and despair.

We are not in the business of excusing the inexcusable.

Nor will we ever be rid of criminals, for they existed long before the current gangs arrived on the scene and will go on preying on the rest of us in the future.

But these gangsters are something else—and we need to understand why.

EVALUATING THE AUTHOR'S ARGUMENT:

In the viewpoint you just read, Richard Williamson strongly condemns the lack of moral values evident among violent gang members. He refers to gang members with terminology that has negative connotations, calling them "young thugs," "soulless killers," and "self-styled outlaws." Does his use of this type of language strengthen his argument? Why or why not?

VIEWPOINT 2

Poor Parenting Causes Gang Violence

A.J. Rossillo

"There is a serious issue of proper parenting— or lack thereof— when young males are allowed to . . . join gangs."

Many commentators and gang experts believe that young people turn to gangs due to a lack of alternatives, such as community programs that offer job training and recreational activities. In the following viewpoint, A.J. Rossillo rejects this argument. Instead, Rossillo insists that joining a gang is simply the result of a bad decision. While youths themselves must be held accountable for making this bad choice, the author argues, the ultimate responsibility lies with parents. Rossillo maintains that it is the duty of parents to teach their children right from wrong and to forcefully prohibit them from joining gangs and breaking laws. Rossillo is a resident of Syracuse, New York, who wrote this viewpoint for the local newspaper.

AS YOU READ, CONSIDER THE FOLLOWING QUESTIONS:

1. Who is responsible for Delmar Everson's death, according to Rossillo?
2. According to the author, why will money for community programs and police not solve the gang violence problem?

In the past few weeks there has been a rash of shootings in Syracuse, two of which have resulted in deaths. A lot of airtime has been dedicated to these events.

As usual at such times, certain people make their way to the forefront in an attempt to point the finger of blame: Family and friends of victims, suspects, esteemed community leaders and reverends raise their arms and voices in anger and disbelief over why this is happening in their communities. There are subtle hints that surely the fault lies beyond that of the person responsible for pulling the trigger. There are demands for more money for "community programs" aimed at curbing violence within the African-American community, where they claim young black males are at risk. Government officials and the police need to care more, and somehow step in to lead certain people to a better life.

FAST FACT

Being a member of a street gang increases a person's risk of violent death by 60 percent.

Why is it that the responsibility for illegal and immoral behavior always seems to fall on someone other than the actor? When was the last time someone on the news pointed the finger where it belonged—at these young kids and their parents? There is a serious issue of proper parenting—or lack thereof—when young males are allowed to hang out on street corners at all hours of the day or night, join gangs and subsequently engage in criminal behavior.

What happened to make it acceptable behavior to hunt down other human beings like animals and kill them? Were they never taught about the consequences of their actions, or the respect for human dignity and life? Is their home life so inadequate and unappealing that they must seek the comfort of a gang? Do they not see or hope for more out of life than drug-dealing and guns? This is a void in their life that needs to be filled by parents, immediate family and true friends, not the government, police or community centers.

The Rev. Larry Ellis claims that one of the victims, Delmar Everson, was a loving father with dreams and aspirations. Early on, Delmar chose a life that got him involved in numerous confrontations with trouble and the police. This was the life he chose to live because it was more appealing than anything else presented to him. He and many others like him died as a direct result of their choice. No one forced him into it, and apparently he wasn't dissuaded from this type of life, either.

His own friend, Jerry Lodman, admits this. He claims Delmar once saved his life by protecting him from being shot. He speaks as if it's nothing out of the ordinary to be shot at. Why did they choose to put themselves in a situation where they were susceptible to violent, criminal activity?

They weren't random victims. Had someone been able to make a significant difference in their lives at an early age, maybe they would have

A tattooed gang member kisses his young son on the head. Some experts contend that the parents are to blame for their children's involvement in gang activity.

Source: Gamble. © 1999 by *The Florida Times-Union*. Reproduced by permission of Ed Gamble.

chosen a different path. Instead, our experts in community leadership wait for the inevitable to happen, then commence with the blame game and cries for justice.

Hundreds of thousands of dollars are spent every year for community programs, police overtime and sensitivity training, in an attempt to reduce violence within a certain portion of the African-American community. Yet no matter how much money is dedicated to this cause, the problem continues.

How much money do we need to spend to raise a child to understand the difference between right and wrong? How much does it cost parents to teach their children that people in a civilized society will not accept criminal and immoral behavior? That there is more dignity in working at McDonald's than hanging out on a corner selling drugs and being involved in gangs?

How much does it take for a parent to teach a child respect toward other human beings and the value of living a good life? Nothing! Zero dollars.

Children and young adults are going to make mistakes. It's part of the learning process. But when they choose to join a gang, pick up a gun and kill someone, the problem goes well beyond being young and not knowing any better. They were greatly lacking in the necessary guidance as they were growing up—guidance within a solid family environment.

We could go back and forth as to who is to blame, what can be done about the violence, how much money needs to be spent to solve the problem. As long as people refuse to take corrective action with their children at an early age, the shootings and homicides will continue. Take control of your children early on and teach them to be proud of who they are and what they can accomplish in life.

Don't like me preaching morality? Then maybe you should—to your kids!

EVALUATING THE AUTHORS' ARGUMENTS:

The viewpoint you just read is an opinion piece written for a community newspaper. The author, A.J. Rossillo, forcefully expresses a personal point of view on the topic but does not rely on outside sources of information to support this perspective. The following article by Beth Barrett is a feature story written by a journalist. The author does not express a strong point of view but instead quotes the views of probation officers and former gang members. As you read Barrett's viewpoint, consider whether it is more or less effective than Rossillo's viewpoint at exposing the true cause of gang violence.

Gang Violence Is Urban Warfare

Beth Barrett

> *"The proliferation of [weapons] . . . mixed with vast sums of money at stake in drug dealing . . . have created ever more incendiary conditions."*

Los Angeles is sometimes referred to as the gang capital of the nation because half of all homicides in the city are gang-related. The following viewpoint is part of an eight-part series of stories on the L.A. gang problem published in the *Los Angeles Daily News* in September 2004. Beth Barrett, a staff writer for the paper, explains that gang violence is the result of a thirty-year history of battles over drug sales territory. The violence is also fueled, she argues, by despair and rage that result from racism, poverty, and a lack of opportunities for youths. Due to these feelings of anger and hopelessness, according to Barrett, gang members are quick to resort to violence when they believe rival gang members have offended them. One act of violence can start a cycle of killing and reprisals that often spirals out of control, creating an atmosphere similar to a war zone in the inner city.

AS YOU READ, CONSIDER THE FOLLOWING QUESTIONS:

1. What question is "Nowhere" no longer the answer to, according to Barrett?

2. According to Scott "Popeye" Rosengard, what are the benefits of gang membership?
3. What do gang members learn from being shot, according to James Dunn?

Revenge mixed with the high-stakes battle for control of drug trafficking drives most gang violence.

An insult, a confrontation, one incident leading to another, creates a seemingly endless cycle of drive-by shootings and street violence that claims the lives of the innocent as well as the gangster.

The toughest streets in the city [Los Angeles] seem like a war zone. Gang members patrol their neighborhoods exacting "taxes" from nongang members who want to sell drugs or work as prostitutes. Addicts mingle with dealers as ordinary people try to steer clear of trouble and go about their lives without incident.

"This is our war on terrorism," said Ronald Preston, 55, an old "Outlaw" gangster known as "Baba" who served 12 years in prison for kidnapping, robbery and attempted murder.

"We face violence every day. We hear gunshots and ambulances every day. This is not arbitrary violence; there is a logic."

His view is echoed by Pete Cavitt, 47, once a kingpin in the East Coast Crips who has seen two of his sons killed and now works as a gang interventionist trying to stop the bloodshed.

"This is a black Civil War in this city that goes back 30 years. It's spread through the city like the plague. There are the haves and the not having, and, simply, if you don't have, the frustration mounts, anger sets in and the least infringement in a neighborhood leads to chaos, revenge killings. No one wins."

Poverty, Racism, and Rage

Tensions between blacks and Latinos, worsening poverty, the lack of good jobs combined with the lingering effects of racism, despair and a host of other problems create the conditions in which joining a gang often provides a sense of belonging that is otherwise lacking.

"This stuff is deeply rooted . . . the rage is deeply within," said Kenny Valentine, 42, a gang intervention specialist with Unity T.W.O. Inc. and former Swans member.

"When you're young, whichever neighborhood you're brought up in, you're poor, there's no field trips, no jobs. That's why they love their neighborhoods so much. If they're disrespected by someone scratching their name on a wall, or someone comes in to mess with a female, that's disrespect. It's totally about respect."

Law enforcement authorities said the proliferation of semiautomatic and automatic weapons and sawed-off shotguns mixed with vast sums of money at stake in drug dealing and other criminal activity and idealization of gangsters in movies and music have created ever more incendiary conditions.

Gangsters aren't bound by codes of conduct that used to exist and provided some sense of orderliness. For example, the answer "Nowhere,"

Facts About Los Angeles Gangs

Southern California

- Number of gangs in Los Angeles County: 1,000

- Number of gang members in Los Angeles County: 80,000–85,000

- Percentage of gang members that are violent: 4% to 10%

- Number of gang-related homicides in Southern California 1999–2004: 3,000

- Cost of each gang-related homicide (including prison costs): $1.75 million

Los Angeles County

- Total costs of gang-related murders from 1999–2004: $5.2 billion

Source: Beth Barrett, "Homegrown Terror," *Los Angeles Daily News,* September 26, 2004.

Poverty and a lack of opportunity drive many youths to join gangs.

to the question "Where you from?" no longer is protection from a gang execution.

"There's no answer (anymore)," said Superior Court Commissioner Jack Gold. "They shoot at them anyway."

Gold, who has dealt with gang members for more than two decades, said he is seeing more young kids, some only 8 or 9, carrying weapons.

The same is true of taggers who "have taken on the persona of gangs in terms of dress . . . and weapons," no longer just spray-painting graffiti.

Recently, Gold said, a fully automatic weapon was found in the home of a teenage SRS Norinco tagging crew member, who had been placed on probation.

"The appeal of gangs and graffiti needs to be addressed at the grammar school level, and it's not."

The Strongest Influence

The point that often is missed, say experts in the field, is that in many poor areas the gangs represent the strongest influence on children, especially boys, as they grow up. Gang leaders are looked up to and imitated and joining a gang is a rite of passage—one that can only lead to "prison or death" without effective intervention, said Scott "Popeye" Rosengard, a veteran probation officer.

"Gang behavior is an addiction. . . . It could be controlled."

Another probation officer, Howard Gold, said treating the addiction requires addressing not only the violent behavior, but also the depression, sadness and hopelessness that drives it.

"Being a gang member today gives status, access to drugs, a girl magnet. There is this view they're the modern-day warriors. You're talking about taking a whole identity away. You have to replace it with something."

Afraid of Nothing

On patrol one summer night, officers spotted a group of teenagers and young men in gang attire arguing in front of an apartment along Vanowen Street.

A Haskell Locos gang member jumped in a car and the cops chased it, radioing their partners to follow up with the gang members still on the street. Officers caught up with the man who drove off and found he had no license and that there was an open beer inside. They called for an impound.

Officers in a second car, back where the chase started, handcuffed Samuel Morales, 21, another Haskell gang member. He was busted in April [2004] with a gun and put on probation. Now, he was carrying a bat, another weapon.

"I'm not afraid of nothing; I'm just not," Morales boasted as the cops prepared to book him. "You're going to die; you're going to die somehow."

A Haskell Street tattoo on his neck, his head shaved, Morales said he's lived in the same apartment all his life; seen his uncle and his friends killed, and has learned to "torture" rivals, just like they "torture" him.

"Every gang member wants to kill you."

Next to him was a 15-year-old boy who officers said had been in a gang for only three weeks. Caught between the cops and Morales, the boy alternately looked defiant and scared. And then his mother arrived.

"I need help," she told the cops.

The boy was taken to the station for booking on a minor offense, which will mean he can be placed on probation—the surest way the officers say some structure can be imposed and any more gang activities stopped.

Gang officers say the hardest part of the job is talking to kids "until you're blue in the face" only to have them killed.

A policeman searches for a suspect during a sting operation. Many officers believe that fearlessness among gang members has led to an increase in violent crimes.

Students of a middle school in Illinois express their frustration with a new school policy banning certain hairstyles. Administrators implemented the policy to help reduce on-campus gang activity.

"A person you just gave this speech to about life a few hours later is choking on their own blood and the family is screaming," said LAPD gang officer Nick Nemecek. "You think about it. It never goes away."

A Long-Running War

The stretch of West 74th Street in front of Pete Cavitt's home in South Los Angeles has flowed with the blood of his friends and his family for the better part of two decades.

In revenge, his East Coast Crips band of brothers have turned streets and avenues nearby into killing fields.

Today, Cavitt, 47, and three of his homeboys are the survivors of a long-running "war" between their Crips set and the Swans, a nearby Bloods gang. Between them, they have spent more than three decades in prison, including time for murder. They bear scars from bullets from the reign of terror they were part of and they share a passionate desire that their sons and daughters be spared any more of this warfare.

"We've buried so much of each other; we've been the death of each other. We're going to have no more of these babies with bullets in their heads," Cavitt said, bending to kiss his granddaughter, the daughter of one of his dead sons.

"It has to end now, right now. We can make it happen in this city."

Cavitt, who has the street handle "Pee Pee" tattooed on the inside of his left forearm along with "East Coast Original Crip," and James Dunn, 42, who earned the nickname "The Godfather" for never backing down, are affiliated with the nonprofit Unity T.W.O., working to defuse tensions.

Dunn spent 10 years in prison and was shot twice, the second time in the summer of 2000 as he went to check on a friend who had been shot—and as it turned out, killed. The bullets remain in his hip, a medal of honor of sorts in the streets.

The new generation, like the old, has grown up conditioned to violence, Dunn said. No one thinks they'll ever be shot, and even after they are, they don't think it will happen again.

"You sort of look at it like, 'Hey, I have to be a little more sharp next time.' Most of the times I got shot there was warning signs, you know. You see the signs—somebody's in your neighborhood who looks shady, funny and then, here they come again. So you say, 'OK, you got caught slipping, you're shot.' You ignored the signs." . . .

"A lot of these youngsters are running around without a clue of what they're doing in the first place," Cavitt said. "You ask them, they can't tell you. If we can enlighten them . . . this isn't even their war. The war is between East Coast and Swans, going on for 30 years; that war is at an end right now."

EVALUATING THE AUTHOR'S ARGUMENT:

In the viewpoint you just read, Beth Barrett compares some areas of Los Angeles to a war zone due to the prevalence of gang violence there. Based on her descriptions and quotes, do you think this comparison is valid or an exaggeration? Support your answer with quotes from the viewpoint.

VIEWPOINT 4

Young People Join Gangs Due to Social Inequality

James Diego Vigil

> *"The street gang is an outcome of . . . the relegation of certain persons or groups to the fringes of society."*

In the following viewpoint James Diego Vigil argues that gangs form as a result of social forces that leave minorities marginalized. Writing specifically about Los Angeles, Vigil contends that minorities face poverty, racism, and discrimination in the public schools. These factors, combined with instability at home, leave many youths disconnected from both society and their families. In response to this alienation, many young people seek solace in street gangs, where they find protection, friendship, and support. Vigil is a professor of social ecology at the University of California, Irvine. He is the author of *Barrio Gangs: Street Life and Identity in Southern California* and *A Rainbow of Gangs: Street Cultures in the Mega-City*, from which this viewpoint was taken.

AS YOU READ, CONSIDER THE FOLLOWING QUESTIONS:

1. What two reasons does Vigil give for the need to examine the role of families, schools, and law enforcement in causing the gang problem?
2. What school policies have worked against minorities, according to the author?
3. What does social order depend on, as outlined by Vigil?

The street gang is an outcome of marginalization, that is, the relegation of certain persons or groups to the fringes of society, where social and economic conditions result in powerlessness. This process occurs on multiple levels as a product of pressures and forces in play over a long period of time. The phrase "multiple marginality" reflects the complexities and persistence of these forces. . . . Forces . . . that occur at the broader levels of society lead to economic insecurity and lack of opportunity, fragmented institutions of social control, poverty, and psychological and emotional barriers among large segments of the ethnic minority communities in Los Angeles. These are communities whose members face inadequate living conditions, stressful personal and family changes, and racism and cultural repression in schools. . . .

Daily strains from many directions take their toll and strip minority peoples of their coping skills. Being left out of mainstream society in so many ways and in so many places relegates these urban youths to the margins of society in practically every sense. This positioning leaves them with few options or resources to better their lives. Often, they seek a place where they are not marginalized—and find it in the streets. Thus, a result of multiple marginalization has

> **FAST FACT**
>
> Joining a gang is usually a ritualized event. The recruit is typically "jumped in." Being jumped in means being severely beaten in order to prove one's toughness and solidarity with the gang. New recruits are also often required to prove their loyalty by committing an act of violence, such as shooting a rival gang member.

been the emergence of street gangs and the generation of gang members. The same kinds of pressures and forces that push male youth into gangs also apply to females.

Society and the criminal justice system have so far not fashioned adequate responses to curtail gang growth. Families, schools, and law enforcement merit special scrutiny in this regard for two main reasons. First, they are the primary agents of social control in society. Second, they are uniquely adaptive and responsive to the concerns of society. Although each of these institutions has made its separate contribution to the gang problem, it is their joint actions (or inactions) that make the problem worse. It is in the vacuum of their collective failure that street socialization has taken over and rooted the quasi institution of the street gang.

Family Disruption

Family life and parenting practices play the initial role in the socialization of a child. It is within the family that individuals form their first significant relationships, and family training first guides and directs them onto a conventional path of participation in society. In short, parents are the primary caretakers who introduce the child to the world. They gradually expand the child's social space (i.e., from the cradle to the bedroom to the home to the neighborhood) to include other, non-kin influences. Disruptions in family life place stress on parenting practices and duties. In poverty-ridden, ethnic minority communities, these disruptions often result in abbreviated or curtailed supervision and direction of household children. Female gang members are often twice affected, since they generally become single parents—"stroller queens," in the words of one flippant observer. Despite the alarming statistics, however, it must be noted that some of these women successfully navigate a life of poverty, mature out of gangs, and become strong and committed mothers.

Minorities Are Poorly Served by Schools

Clearly, educational institutions serve as society's primary arena for turning out citizens and trained members of the workforce. In the United States, schools are next in importance to the family in providing structure and meaning to children's lives and acting as an agency for social control. As a child grows up, schools eventually assume the responsibilities of the family for the bulk of each child's daytime activities. . . .

A young boy walks along a garbage-covered street in an inner-city neighborhood in Washington, D.C. Some experts argue that a lack of opportunities in such areas leads youths to join gangs.

Some commentaters believe that poor schools contribute to gang membership among low-income and minority students.

Low-income and ethnic minorities have historically suffered negative, damaging experiences in the educational system. Research shows that standard school policies such as tracking by ability group and the use of standardized tests as the ultimate measure of educational performance and ability have worked against minority students. These students often attend segregated, underfunded, inferior schools, where they encounter cultural insensitivity and an ethnocentric curriculum.

The motivation and strategies for seeking a higher status begin in the family but are formally forged in the educational system and process. In complex societies, schools serve as the mechanism for youths to translate their aspirations into conventional, constructive goals. In terms of reaching for a higher status, many low-income children exhibit a gap between aspirations and expectations. Even though they might have high hopes, they are led (often unaware) to see their goals as outside of their world, exceeding their grasp. Being pragmatic, they assume they won't realize their dreams.

The Role of Law Enforcement

The acceptance of the "rightness" of the central social value system is pivotal to social control and citizenship, for individuals are obviously more likely to break the rules if they do not believe in the rules and regulations. Social order depends on the personal internalization of the values of society (the "ought-tos") and of patterned behavior that adheres to the norms of society (the blueprints for action). The latter are first and primarily inculcated by parents, followed by schools, and reinforced early on by peers, especially during the passage from childhood to adulthood.

Youths who are weakly (or not at all) tethered to home and school have weakened ties to society's conventional institutions and values. Because of this deficit, members of law enforcement—the street social-control specialists—often step in as the controlling authority of last resort for our youth. Law enforcement and the criminal justice apparatus serve as the sanctioning source for individuals who consistently fail to conform. When they enter the picture, it is clear that society has not only failed to properly integrate its low-income members but additionally . . . is making it easier for them to become street-socialized.

Street Socialization

Multiple forces working jointly lead to children spending more time on the streets, under the purview and guidance of a multiple-aged peer group. In various Los Angeles ethnic communities, this group often takes the form of the street gang. For girls as well as boys, the street becomes a haven and gang life is romanticized, even though it often ultimately brings them trouble and, for girls, additional victimization. What established gangs in the neighborhood have to offer is nurture, protection, friendship, emotional support, and other ministrations for unattended, unchaperoned resident youth. In other words, street socialization fills the voids left by inadequate parenting and schooling, especially inadequate familial care and supervision. This street-based process molds the youth to conform to the ways of the street. On the streets, the person acquires the models and means for new norms, values, and attitudes. . . .

Dropout rates for ethnic minorities, especially for Latinos and African Americans, are notoriously high, and the children most affected are the street-based ones: In some South Central Los Angeles high schools, the rates are as high as 79 percent. Once out of school, the students drop into gangs and commit to the gang's values and norms.

Street socialization alienates youths from what is learned in the schools, while societal discrimination and economic injustice further erode allegiance to conventional commitments. Boys and girls from these backgrounds are regularly truant from school and organize "ditching parties," a practice that reinforces "we-ness" among street peers. (Ditching parties are get-togethers, often to share drinks or drugs, by adolescents who are "ditching," i.e., illicitly not attending school.) With such a weak educational foundation, coupled with family voids, it is no wonder that a conventional path to a higher status escapes the purview of most gang members. Generally poor job prospects exacerbate the situation for minority youth who already have family and school difficulties.

Through the marginalization and street socialization of urban youth and the creation of a street gang subculture, with values and norms of its own, the street gang becomes a subsociety. Once this subsociety has been created to meet the needs of its creators, it persists and becomes an urban fixture in certain neighborhoods, compelling future generations of youth to join it or otherwise come to terms with it. In these ways, at home and in schools, urban youth acquire a gang-oriented set of rules and regulations.

EVALUATING THE AUTHORS' ARGUMENTS:

Throughout this chapter, authors have cited various reasons why young people join gangs and commit gang-related violence. Some emphasize social forces, while others stress the individual gang member's responsibility. List all of the causes of gang violence mentioned in this chapter and rank them from the most important to least important. Explain why you ordered them the way you did.

CHAPTER 3

How Can Gang Violence Be Reduced?

An incarcerated member of the L.A. Crips flashes his gang sign from a jail cell.

Aggressive Law Enforcement Is Needed to Reduce Gang Violence

Syracuse Post-Standard

"Arrest the bad guys, convict them and put them in prison."

In cities and localities across the United States, law enforcement officials are given the task of responding to the problem of gang violence. The following viewpoint is an editorial originally published in the *Syracuse Post-Standard*. The editors of the newspaper applaud recent efforts by the police, district attorney, and mayor to crack down on violent gang members. The editors concede that law enforcement is not the only means of addressing the gang problem. They advocate the continuation of efforts to correct the root causes of gang violence, such as poverty and drug abuse. However, they conclude, strong law enforcement is essential in order to catch violent gang members and remove them from society before they can do more harm.

AS YOU READ, CONSIDER THE FOLLOWING QUESTIONS:
  1. Why have law enforcement officials refrained from using the word *gangs,* according to the authors?
  2. Why is it important to set high bail for gang members who have been taken into custody and charged with crimes, according to the *Post-Standard?*

For social scientists, studying the pathologies of urban gangs is a complex and challenging academic pursuit.

For people who live in the neighborhoods where gangs operate, the issue is more basic.

They don't want to get shot.

They don't want their kids to get shot.

They want to live in peace, without the uninterrupted fear that they or someone they love will step into the path of a bullet.

It is that more fundamental question that inspires an initiative by the Syracuse Police Department and the Onondaga County District Attorney's office. The people who work there are not social scientists; their job is to put an end to the mayhem, to make the streets secure for law-abiding people to go about their lives in peace.

Police Chief Dennis DuVal put it succinctly: "This is about saving lives in our community. This is not about any politics or anything else."

Arrest the bad guys, convict them and put them in prison. It may not do much to address the social roots of the gang culture. But it gets guns

> **FAST FACT**
>
> In October 2000 the Rand Corporation, a public policy research organization, began an intervention to prevent gang violence in Hollenbeck, a particularly violent area of East Los Angeles. Rand's strategy, which included increased police patrols and gun-law enforcement, led to a 32 percent decrease in gang-related violence.

and shooters off the streets. There are lots of guns and lots of shooters, and the police can't get them all. But any reduction in the carnage is worth pursuing. Any life saved is worth the effort.

A police officer arrests a suspected gang member in Los Angeles. Some people argue that aggressive law enforcement is the most effective response to the gang problem.

This represents a significant change in approach for the local law-enforcement community. In the past, the police have been reluctant to utter the "G-word" for the record, not wanting to aggrandize the exploits of these urban terrorists. This new frankness is refreshing, and it promises to be more effective in reducing violence. People in the neighborhoods already know about the gangs. They need to know that police and prosecutors think they're safety is worth protecting.

Anticipating complaints about defendants' rights, District Attorney William Fitzpatrick promised that proper arrest and prosecution procedures would be observed carefully. Fitzpatrick has created a task force of five lawyers to prosecute gang cases. He has promised speedy indictment and trial of defendants.

This strategy makes sense. The object, after all, is to gain convictions and long prison sentences for offenders, not to have cases thrown out or convictions reversed because the rights of defendants were not safeguarded.

DuVal, Fitzpatrick and Syracuse Mayor Matt Driscoll emphasized that they need the assistance of law-abiding citizens in this effort. This will require no small amount of courage on their part. Reprisals and intimidation of witnesses are always a threat when gangs are involved. Toward that end, Fitzpatrick has called upon judges to set bail high enough so defendants aren't released to harass and threaten witnesses against them.

None of this means that government, and the society that supports it, shouldn't address the root causes of gang violence—drug abuse, poverty, despair, moral aimlessness. There are a lot of resources already devoted to that in Syracuse, and there have been positive results. Those efforts must continue. Indeed, they should be increased.

But that's not the mission of police and prosecutors. Their job is to identify those committing crimes against their neighbors, arrest them, prosecute them. Their job is to protect innocent people against the immediate deadly peril. Their job, literally and metaphorically, is to stop the bleeding.

EVALUATING THE AUTHORS' ARGUMENTS:

In the viewpoint you just read, the editors of the *Syracuse Post-Standard* acknowledge the need to address the "root causes" of gang violence, but they place more emphasis on the importance of law enforcement. In the next viewpoint, the editors of the *Los Angeles Daily News* agree that law enforcement is part of the solution, but they place more importance on the need to solve the social problems that they say cause gang violence. After you have read both articles, what approach do you think is best—more law enforcement, more efforts to solve social problems, or some combination of both?

Aggressive Law Enforcement Alone Will Not Reduce Gang Violence

Los Angeles Daily News

"The 'war on gangs' has produced the exact opposite of its intended results."

The following viewpoint is an editorial that was written by the editors of the *Los Angeles Daily News*. The editors argue that in the effort to combat gangs, law enforcement is not enough. In fact, according to the editors, an excessive emphasis on law enforcement has made the gang problem worse in Los Angeles. By applying intense police pressure to the problem, the city has alienated law-abiding citizens who might otherwise cooperate in antigang efforts. Also, the city has overlooked other, more fruitful ways to counter the gang problem. Rather than relying primarily on law enforcement, community leaders and politicians should work to solve the cultural problems—such as widespread fatherlessness and media glorification of violence—that allow gangs to thrive.

AS YOU READ, CONSIDER THE FOLLOWING QUESTIONS:
1. By what factor has the number of gang members in Los Angeles multiplied since 1975, as reported by the *Daily News*?
2. What percentage of gang members are responsible for the most damage, according to the authors?
3. According to the *Daily News,* who must play a role in defeating gangs?

There's a reason why Southern California's three-decade-long war against gang violence has failed, and it's not because we're not trying hard enough.

It's because, for too long, we've relied on all the wrong strategies. . . .

Gangs and gang violence are not law enforcement problems alone. And that has been the focus of our region's strategy. The effort, though often underfunded yet intense at times, has resulted in an outcome that has been nothing short of disastrous.

The "war on gangs" has produced the exact opposite of its intended results. It's made gangsters more brazen, not less; more ruthless, more

Paramedics stabilize a Los Angeles gang member who was shot during a gang-related shooting.

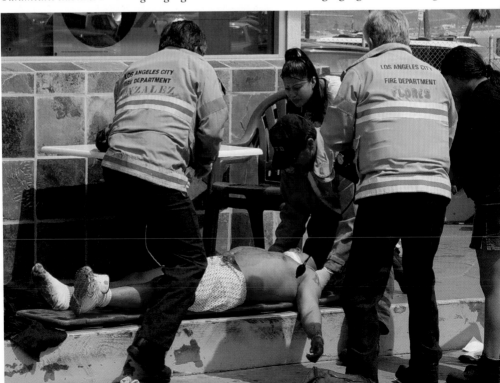

cruel, more indifferent to the suffering they inflict. It's caused their numbers to swell, not shrink. Since 1975, when the Los Angeles Police Department first launched elite anti-gang units, the number of gangsters in the region has multiplied tenfold.

This is not progress. It is spectacular failure. And it ought to prompt some serious rethinking of our policies, our social structures, our attitudes, even the very way we lead our lives.

Where have we gone wrong?

A Simplistic Solution

The key word is "we." For too long, society has viewed gangs as an "inner-city" problem, something of little consequence, let alone responsibility, for those of us in ostensibly safer ZIP codes. We have allowed impacted communities to suffer alone, while their pathologies have spilled out across the region. Now, no neighborhood is safe.

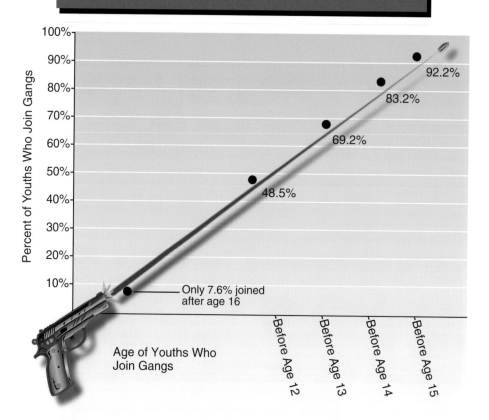

At What Age Do Most Youths Join Gangs?

Percent of Youths Who Join Gangs

100%
90% — 92.2%
80% — 83.2%
70% — 69.2%
60%
50%
40% — 48.5%
30%
20%
10% — Only 7.6% joined after age 16

Age of Youths Who Join Gangs

Before Age 12 Before Age 13 Before Age 14 Before Age 15

Source: From a survey of 1,042 incarcerated gang members conducted by the National Gang Crime Research Center.

A gang member poses with weapons and cash. Some commentators insist that the war on gangs has only served to make gang members more ruthless and brazen in their activities.

We have treated all gang members like urban terrorists, when really only 4 percent to 10 percent of them are responsible for most of the damage. This failure to discriminate has kept us from applying the maximum amount of pressure on the most hardened of criminals. It's also prevented us from offering a way out to those gang members who are eager, but unable, to put the criminal life behind them.

Worse yet, indiscriminate police sweeps have made entire neighborhoods come to view cops, not as friends, but as enemies. Potential informants have gone silent, and gangs have easily preyed on young recruits who know of nowhere else to find security.

Our simplistic perceptions have led us to pursue a simplistic solution, treating the gang problem as merely a law enforcement issue, when what was needed, along with tough policing, was a full-scale cultural assault.

In trying to smack down "gangsters" as a single monolith, we've failed to reach out with real alternatives for individual people, to inspire hope and opportunity among those who are dispirited. We've neglected to deal adequately with social root causes, like rampant fatherlessness, which leads too many young men to find male role models in all the wrong places.

And, through our popular culture and entertainment media, we have sent out the message that cruelty and lawlessness are cool; hope and responsibility are not.

To defeat gangs, police must play a key role, but so must social workers, the clergy, schools, the media, parents, siblings and friends. Each and every one of us—in the attitudes we hold, the choices we make, even the products we buy—helps to shape the culture that must be unified in its commitment to making our neighborhoods safer.

EVALUATING THE AUTHOR'S ARGUMENTS:

In the viewpoint you just read, the editors of the *Los Angeles Daily News* suggest that many people have ignored the gang problem because they view it as an inner-city problem that does not affect them. Do you agree? Why or why not? Does your community have a gang presence? If so, do you believe the authorities are addressing the issue adequately? Why or why not?

VIEWPOINT 3

Antiloitering Laws Can Help Reduce Gang Violence

Dan M. Kahan and Tracey L. Meares

"Supporters of the Chicago gang-loitering law saw it as a way to secure order without destroying the lives of the community youth."

In recent years, many cities have sought new ways to prevent gang violence. One solution has been to pass laws that prohibit gang members from congregating in public places. The reasoning behind these laws, often called antiloitering laws, is that by breaking up groups of idle young people and removing them from the streets, authorities can prevent them from committing crime and violence.

Although these laws have been created with good intentions, they have been harshly criticized. Opponents argue that the laws violate young people's constitutional right to freely associate and be protected by due process of law. One such law, in Chicago, was challenged all the way to the U.S. Supreme Court. In the 1999 case of *Chicago v. Morales,* the Court overturned the law on the grounds that it granted too much discretion to police officers in determining whom to disperse and arrest.

In the following viewpoint, Dan M. Kahan and Tracey L. Meares argue that despite the

Dan M. Kahan and Tracey L. Meares, "Public-Order Policing Can Pass Constitutional Muster," *The Wall Street Journal,* June 15, 1999, p. A18. Copyright © 1999 by Dow Jones & Company, Inc. All rights reserved. Reproduced by permission of the publisher and authors.

Court's ruling in *Chicago v. Morales,* antiloitering ordinances and similar laws are a good idea. In fact, the authors maintain, the minority community supports such laws because they allow society to remove young people from the streets before they are drawn into gang behavior, which often leads to their death and imprisonment. According to Kahan and Meares, the Supreme Court's ruling did not forbid antiloitering laws but rather provided guidelines for how they should be written in order to be deemed constitutional. Therefore, they conclude, new laws should be developed.

Dan M. Kahan is a professor at Yale Law School. Tracey L. Meares is the Max Pam Professor of Law and the director of the Center for Studies in Criminal Justice at the University of Chicago Law School. Kahan and Meares are the coauthors of the book *Urgent Times: Policing and Rights in Inner-City Communities.*

AS YOU READ, CONSIDER THE FOLLOWING QUESTIONS:

1. For what purpose were "public-order" laws used in the United States prior to the 1960s, as related by the authors?
2. How could the Chicago antiloitering law have been made constitutional, according to Kahan and Meares?

L ast Thursday [June 10, 1999] the Supreme Court, by a vote of 6-3, struck down Chicago's loitering law, which aimed to curtail the activities of street gangs. The law was part of a nationwide revolution in policing: From Boston to Dallas, from Miami to Los Angeles, cities are heeding the demand of minority residents for policing strategies aimed at restoring order to inner-city streets. The question isn't whether this revolution will continue, but only what form it must take to satisfy the Constitution.

Chicago's gang-loitering law authorized police to disperse groups of gang members when they gathered on city streets with "no apparent purpose." Objecting to the discretion that the law appeared to confer upon the police, the court struck the law down as unconstitutional.

Minority Support

To be sure, antiloitering laws, curfews and similar public-order provisions have a checkered history. Before the civil-rights reforms of the

Police cameras (inset) set up in busy urban areas of Chicago monitor city streets in an effort to help police prevent gang activity.

1960s, police forces in both the North and South selectively enforced such laws against minorities. But the new public-order provisions, of which the Chicago law was only one example, have a very different political pedigree. They have been enacted at the behest of minority inner-city dwellers, who see them as tolerably moderate alternatives to severe prison sentences for nonviolent offenders.

Neil Bosanko, one of the supporters of the Chicago law, is typical. Mr. Bosanko heads the South Chicago Chamber of Commerce, an organization that includes some 275 civic, church and business groups on Chicago's impoverished and largely African-American South Side. Not surprisingly, Mr. Bosanko resents intimidating displays of gang authority, which impair the South Side's economic vitality.

Mr. Bosanko also has a more personal reason to support preventive policing strategies: His own son is serving a life prison term for his involvement in a gang-style murder. Mr. Bosanko and other supporters of the Chicago gang-loitering law saw it as a way to secure order without destroying the lives of the community youth who find themselves enmeshed in the social and economic forces that fuel gang criminality.

FAST FACT

In addition to antiloitering laws, many cities have instituted gang injunctions. These laws prohibit known gang members from gathering in public with other known gang members. Los Angeles has seventeen injunctions on the books targeted at specific gangs.

The same complex of motivations has fueled minority political support for curfews in Dallas and Miami, antigang nuisance laws in Los Angeles and innovative community-centered policing in Boston and other cities. The inner-city residents who support the new public-order laws are not entrenched insiders bent on harassing despised outsiders. Rather, they are the mothers and fathers, sisters and brothers, neighbors and friends of the very people whom these laws most directly affect. They realize that it's much better to give the police the authority to order kids off the streets tonight than to leave the police no choice but to haul these same kids off to jail tomorrow.

In June 1999 the Supreme Court struck down Chicago's antiloitering law, an ordinance that resulted in the arrests of this man and many others who remained on the streets past curfew.

These citizens are also far from indifferent to police brutality. For that reason, they frequently insist that community policing initiatives be accompanied by administrative checks to ensure that the police exercise discretion in an accountable and responsible fashion.

Creating a Constitutional Law

The support of minorities for public-order provisions doesn't by itself imply that such policing techniques are constitutional, of course. But it does suggest that it would be a mistake for courts to view such laws with the same suspicion they appropriately afforded to an earlier generation of public-order laws, the obvious purpose of which was to visit special burdens on minorities.

Nothing in the Supreme Court's recent decision on the Chicago gang-loitering law is to the contrary. For technical reasons, the Court had to confine its attention to the text of the Chicago gang-loitering law; it couldn't take into account the city's administrative safeguards designed to ensure that police would enforce the law only to prevent intimidating displays of gang authority. Had those guidelines been written into the text of the law, the Court would have upheld it. In a concurring opinion, Justice Sandra Day O'Connor (joined by Justice Stephen Breyer) made clear that a law expressly aimed at preventing gangs from "establish[ing] control over identifiable areas" would pass constitutional muster. Presumably the three dissenters would agree.

Accordingly, the Court's decision should be viewed not as a barrier but as a guide to preserving public order. The task now is for cities to enact laws that satisfy the reasonably straightforward dictates the justices have set forth for reconciling the community-policing revolution with the dictates of the Constitution.

EVALUATING THE AUTHORS' ARGUMENTS:

In the viewpoint you just read, the authors' main argument for antiloitering laws is that minority communities approve of such ordinances. In the next viewpoint the author contends that antiloitering laws cause discord between minority communities and the police. Which author is more persuasive on this issue, and why?

Antiloitering Laws Are Ineffective

Thomas M. Keane

"Anti-loitering laws undermine community policing, the highly successful strategy that has revolutionized law enforcement."

In an attempt to crack down on gang violence, various cities have passed laws that prohibit gang members from gathering in public spaces such as street corners and parks. These laws have been criticized for violating several constitutional rights, including the right to due process. In 1999, the Supreme Court ruled that an antiloitering law in Chicago was unconstitutional, leaving the future of such laws in doubt.

In the following viewpoint Thomas M. Keane argues against the use of antiloitering laws as a solution to the problem of gang violence. Citing a new antiloitering law in the city of Somerville, Massachusetts, he contends that such laws unfairly target minorities. In addition, he maintains, antiloitering laws are ineffective because they undermine the efforts of police to develop the trust of the community.

Thomas M. Keane, who is a partner at a New York–based equity fund, writes a regular op-ed column for the *Boston Herald* newspaper. He is the recipient of a law degree from

Virginia Law School. From 1993 to 1999 he was a Boston city counselor, and he has extensive experience in business management and financing.

AS YOU READ, CONSIDER THE FOLLOWING QUESTIONS:
  1. What practical problem do antiloitering laws face, according to the author?
  2. What is the idea behind community policing, as outlined by Keane?
  3. What point do you think cartoonist Chuck Asay is making in his cartoon that appears on page ninety-one?

Stunned by a sudden rise in gang violence, politicians in Somerville [a city in Massachusetts] have latched on to a controversial solution: anti-loitering laws. Meanwhile, other nearby communities reject that approach.

Who's right? Not Somerville.

A Quick Fix

Looking for a quick fix, the city of 77,000 has adopted a tactic that police elsewhere believe not only is ineffective, but can backfire—exacerbating, not solving, the gang problem.

Recent gang activity in Somerville has been unquestionably disturbing. About a year ago [in 2002], police in the largely white, blue-collar city became aware of a violent and scary Salvadoran gang called MS13. Last October [2002], gang members allegedly raped two girls. Shockingly, both were handicapped; both deaf, one in a wheelchair. The cruelty of the crimes created enormous pressure on local politicians.

And they reacted quickly. In December the Board of Aldermen passed legislation prohibiting gangs from congregating on streets, sidewalks and in other public places. Mayor Dorothy Kelly Gay signed it. But because it affects criminal codes, the measure still needs approval from the state Legislature.

The new law—the first on the East Coast, say officials—has raised objections from many quarters. For one, anti-loitering laws have an ignoble history. They often have been used to go after groups that were unpopular, unwanted or simply of the wrong ethnic or racial background. Indeed, it was those flaws that caused the U.S. Supreme Court in 1999 to strike down a Chicago ordinance like the one Somerville adopted.

And the fact that the law is clearly targeted at one ethnic group—in this case, Latinos—has prompted cries of profiling. It's hard not to

A street sign warns against gang loitering on a street in the town of Cicero, Illinois. Antiloitering ordinances in the United States have a controversial history.

share those concerns. Bruins [Boston's professional hockey team] players hanging out on a Somerville street corner would not be threatened with imprisonment; Latino males would be. Moreover, says state Rep. Eugene O'Flaherty (D-Chelsea), anti-loitering laws run headlong into a practical problem: Kids like to hangout together. They need to go somewhere.

Not the Way to Prevent Gangs

Yet these issues aside, anti-loitering laws would still be popular if they actually reduced crime.

In Somerville, aldermen concluded that "current laws are inadequate" to deal with gangs. Police Chief George McLean concurs, calling anti-loitering laws a "necessary tool."

Law enforcement officials elsewhere disagree—and their opinions carry weight. For unlike Somerville (where gang activity is a recent phenomenon), Revere, Lynn, East Boston, Chelsea and Winthrop [all cities in Massachusetts] have long experience in dealing with gangs.

> **FAST FACT**
>
> During the three years that Chicago's antiloitering law was in effect (1992 to 1995), nearly 40,000 people were arrested for loitering. Most of them were African Americans and Latinos, according to the American Civil Liberties Union.

"Every police chief I speak to says (anti-loitering legislation) is not the way to go about preventing gang violence," said state Sen. Jarrett Barrios (D-Cambridge), whose district covers Chelsea, Revere and part of Somerville.

Chelsea, for example, recently has been holding hearings on its own anti-loitering measure. Yet even its principal sponsor, City Councilor Paul Nowicki, now seems dubious. And with a strong anti-gang program already in place, police Chief Frank Garvin is skeptical about anti-loitering laws.

So too is Boston's police commissioner, Paul Evans, who worries about "knee-jerk" reactions to crime. "We have little use for laws that target young people," he says. "That's not the way we do things in Boston."

Source: Asay. © 1996 by Creators Syndicate, Inc. Reproduced by permission.

Reverting to the Bad Old Days

The reason is that anti-loitering laws undermine community policing, the highly successful strategy that has revolutionized law enforcement over the last decade.

The old model of policing saw cops as something like a paramilitary force. Oftentimes, that alienated residents, turning crime-fighting into an us-vs.-them confrontation.

The idea behind community policing was to reverse that and make public safety a collaborative process—one that involved the entire community. It meant getting police out of their vehicles and onto the streets where they could get to know residents. It meant working with local churches, charities and other nonprofits to identify troublemakers and try to steer them in a different direction. It meant taking seriously small matters so that they wouldn't escalate.

For many in law enforcement, the newly proposed anti-loitering laws feel like a reversion to the bad old days. They have the potential of pitting the police against the people. They weaken the trust that has been built up between the cops and Latino and other communities.

And, they don't do anything to address the underlying causes of why kids join gangs in the first place.

Are there other approaches? Sure. Chelsea's Councilor Nowicki and police Chief Garvin tick off possibilities: Increase penalties for minor crimes, such as graffiti, when they are committed by gang members. Hold parents responsible for their children's behavior. Evict public housing tenants if they commit crimes as part of a gang. Focus on dampening gang recruitment.

But anti-loitering laws? That approach, says Boston's Evans, "only gets you into trouble."

EVALUATING THE AUTHOR'S ARGUMENTS:

The author of this viewpoint lists several measures that he says would prevent gang violence more effectively than antiloitering laws. What approaches does he list? Do you agree that these efforts are more effective than antiloitering laws? Why or why not?

Parents Can Help Prevent Gang Violence

Valerie Wiener

"To help save their children from youth gangs, parents must make a commitment to their kids."

Valerie Wiener is an author, speaker, and corporate consultant. She is the author of *Gang Free: Friendship Choices for Today's Youth* and *Winning the War Against Youth Gangs: A Guide for Teens, Families, and Communities,* from which this viewpoint was taken. Wiener argues that parents can play a crucial role in keeping young people from joining gangs. She insists that parents must watch for signs that their children may be involved in a gang. In addition, parents need to set a good example and communicate openly with their children.

AS YOU READ, CONSIDER THE FOLLOWING QUESTIONS:

1. When forced to choose between their biological families and their gangs, why do most choose their biological families, according to the author?
2. Name three signs of gang membership cited by Wiener.
3. What suggestions does the author make to help parents get more involved in their children's lives?

One of the most difficult challenges confronting today's families is the influence of youth gangs in their children's lives. As youth gangs grow in presence and dominance, it is now more important than ever for families—especially parents—to get involved in reclaiming their children.

The Youth Gang as "Family"

Many presumptions are floating around that assert that youths involved with gangs do not care about their own biological families. In most situations, this is far from true. In fact, for many youth gangsters, it is the threat of violence to their families—from their gang and others—that prompts them to join the gang in the first place.

Many gang members conceal their membership from their parents because they say it is "easier" on their mothers. They believe that this concealment will keep their moms from worrying about them. As for the parents, many of them deny their child's involvement in a gang, preferring to believe that the child is just mixed up with the wrong crowd.

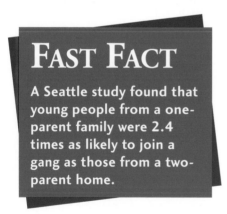

FAST FACT

A Seattle study found that young people from a one-parent family were 2.4 times as likely to join a gang as those from a two-parent home.

Scott H. Decker and Barrik Van Winkle, in *Life in the Gang: Family, Friends and Violence* (1996), measure the relative importance of the gang and the family by asking youth gang members to choose between them. In a study they conducted among gang members, youths turned to their gangs to provide them with things like money and support for involvement in crime. This influence coincides with the youth's natural distancing from family that occurs during adolescence. It is compounded, however, by the extraordinary influence and authority that the gang asserts with negative, and illegal, behaviors.

The Biological Family Is More Important

However, in that same study, eighty-nine percent of those responding said that if forced to choose, they would select their biological

Source: Ramirez. © 2002 by Copley News Service. Reproduced by permission.

family over their gang. The two most frequent reasons for this choice were (1) "The family cares for me more" and (2) "Blood relations are more important than gang affiliations."

When youths are forced to choose between their gangs and their families, something significant takes place. They must weigh competing values in their lives. For most members, gang life provides a place to find protection, companionship, and understanding. Their families, however, represent something even deeper: a commitment, with history—birth, nurturing, caring, support, and love—that surpasses what they have with their gang. Most gang members concede that the family attributes associated with gangs—caring, understanding, and financial support—do not run the depth of commitment that the biological family offers.

One compelling statistic from the Decker and Van Winkle study indicates that ninety-eight percent of youths currently involved in gangs would not want their son or daughter to join one. Most of these respondents described the violence associated with gang membership as a reason to keep their child from joining a gang.

Levels of Parental Involvement

For some parents, the awareness that their child is a gang member produces a natural feeling of anger and even jealousy directed toward the gang. They feel that the gang has taken their child away from them. Parental responses to their child's youth gang involvement vary.

Some parents—*family-first* parents—immerse themselves in an effort to assist their child and to restore the family. Putting the child and the situation first is a healthy way to address the youth gang problem.

Others—*rescuers*—commit themselves to a mission of saving their child while at the same time, minimizing their own fear and accountability. In the short term, the rescue mode can help the child because it involves family support, which also helps the parents through the adjustment process.

Crusaders—those who consider the project to save their children an obsession—often attempt to save other youths as well. While attempting to save everyone, these parents often suppress the root issues with their own children.

Still others—*negators*—know that they themselves have contributed to their child's joining a gang. They tend to respond more negatively. Their common responses include denial that the child is in trouble and denial of responsibility for the child's poor social, emotional,

Las Vegas residents march together to voice their opposition to recent gang-related shootings.

and spiritual well-being. Or, negators might accept the reality of the situation and be unwilling to help the child.

At the extreme are *detached* parents—those who just do not care. These parents refuse to participate in any opportunity to disengage their children from youth gangs.

Whatever the parents believe—and commit to—in attempting to disengage their children from gangs, the process can be more than difficult. Sometimes disengagement requires extreme measures, such as moving away. . . .

Looking for the Signs

No matter how difficult it is, parents and families need to face the reality that gangs are here to stay. Denying this fact would serve no one, especially those children who are vulnerable to joining them. To help reclaim their children or, hopefully, to prevent them from joining gangs, parents need to pay attention to the following signs:

- *Clothes.* Does the child have many clothes of the same color, or certain color combinations, such as black and blue or black and gold? This may indicate gang interest or involvement.
- *Jewelry.* Does the child wear a lot of gold jewelry? Is this jewelry similar to that worn by gangs? How did the child purchase it? Where did that money come from?
- *Money.* Does the child have large—and unaccounted for—amounts of money?
- *Pagers and portable phones.* Does the child really need to have a pager or phone? Does the child use it excessively and privately, especially in places and at times when normal social calls would not occur?
- *Gang symbols.* Does the child have gang symbols on schoolbooks, notebooks, clothes, and/or tattoos?
- *Language.* Does the child use special language, slang, or gang jargon to communicate?
- *Attitude.* Does the child exhibit an unfamiliar, an inappropriate, and a negative attitude about things at home, school, and elsewhere?

A police officer stands over the grave of a slain gang member buried in a Pittsburgh cemetery as he warns a group of troubled youths that a similar fate awaits them if they fail to change their ways.

- *School performance and attendance.* Is the child's school performance sliding for no obvious reason? Has the child been repeatedly truant? Does the child violate curfew laws?
- *Friends.* Does the child "hang out" with people who all wear the same gang-related colors, speak in gang jargon, use gang

signs, listen to the same distressful or violent music, carry weapons, get into trouble with the law, and engage in other irresponsible behavior?

Making a Commitment to the Kids

Certainly it is not just parents and families who want gang-free communities. However, families have the most to lose when gangs do claim their children. To help save their children from youth gangs, parents must make a commitment to their kids. I recommend that you, the parent, do as much as possible of the following, and the more, the better.

Serve as a positive role model. Know that your child watches what you say and do. You are often the first person your child models. Remember how important this can be, and make the best of it.

Get involved in your child's life . . . completely. Many children have excessive amounts of unstructured, unsupervised time. When possible, participate in positive activities with your child. Attend school functions. And show interest in your child's life by asking questions such as: Where are you going? When will you be home? Who are you going with? What's your favorite music group? What do you know about gangs? Do you know how much we love you and need you in this family? One caution: ask in a style that does not sound like an interrogation. Reassure your child that your home is their home. . . .

Monitor your child's progress in school. Repeated truancy makes your child vulnerable to gang recruitment and peer pressure. Check with school attendance officers periodically to ensure that your child is attending school. Encourage your child's commitment to school and offer assistance with projects and homework. . . .

Create positive, family-based alternatives. Organize and implement week-end activities with the family. Find ways to involve members more often. When planning, include suggestions from the child/children you are trying to protect from youth gangs. . . .

Communicate with other parents. Build parental networks that help you help each other. When you share ideas with other parents, you can work collectively and creatively to resolve many issues. This can also help build a friendship network for your child. . . .

Communicate openly and honestly with your child. More than *speaking at* your child, learn to *listen to* your child. *Really* listen. Be willing to listen to your child's concerns and to share yours. Even if your off-spring has joined a gang, do everything possible to keep the lines of communication open. When you say something, mean it and follow through with what you promise, but do not promise more than you can deliver. In fact, underpromise and overdeliver, whenever possible. Work rigorously to establish and grow *trust* in the relationship with your child. Certainly love and support also have a critical place in relationship building between parents and their children. . . .

Other areas of necessary involvement . . . include, but are not limited to: participation in neighborhood watch programs, involvement with school and law enforcement programs and policies related to youth gangs, and interaction with community-wide youth programs and activities.

Making Real Choices

Of all the hard lessons parents can teach their children, one of the hardest is a direct one: Face reality. How critical this lesson is in the life of a youth gangster. Part of this mandate requires that youths accept responsibility for their own behavior—for the choices they make.

Parents must learn how to distinguish between behavior and identity. This means that "what the child *does*" is not the same as "who the child *is*." Therefore, when the child performs poorly, parents must address the specific behavior, not attack the character of the child. The real identity of the child, therefore, is the "who" of that person, and not the "what" performed by the child.

When teaching children about choices, parents should teach them that life is filled with actions—and reactions. They have total control over how they react to things that happen to them. This is the part of their lives where they can make *real choices*. Knowing and taking advantage of this reality gives children genuine power and control over their lives to assert themselves in positive, productive ways.

QUESTIONS FOR DISCUSSION:

In his cartoon that appears on page ninety-five, cartoonist Michael Ramirez depicts gangs as the grim reaper surrounded by darkness and holding a small child. What point do you think he is making with this imagery? Do you think the cartoon is effective? Why or why not?

The Community Must Act to End Gang Violence

Kerman Maddox

"The violence is so great and the loss of life so significant that we all need to set aside our differences and focus on solutions."

In the following viewpoint Kerman Maddox argues that the African American community has not done enough to address the problem of black gang members killing one another. Writing specifically about the situation in Los Angeles, Maddox criticizes the black community for failing to mobilize itself to solve the problem. He calls on black leaders to put aside their differences of opinion and unite in an antiviolence effort that would include parents, churches, and civil rights activists. Kerman Maddox is a political consultant and business owner who teaches political science at Los Angeles Southwest College. He is a member of the board of directors of First African Methodist Episcopal Church, the oldest black church in Los Angeles.

AS YOU READ, CONSIDER THE FOLLOWING QUESTIONS:
1. How did the community respond to Lee Denmon III's murder, according to Maddox?
2. What do parents and church leaders need to do, in the author's opinion?
3. To what California political event does Maddox refer to support his view that the problem of gang violence can be stopped if the public wills it?

Among all the senseless killings in L.A. County, there's one I can't seem to get out of my mind.

Lee Denmon, my former student at Los Angeles Southwest College, was a charming young man and a good student. He respected his elders, stayed out of trouble, worked hard, studied diligently and graduated from college. Then, wanting to help others follow his path, he returned to his community, Inglewood, with dreams of making a difference.

Instead, Denmon became at 23 another ugly statistic in the war of young black men against other young black men.

Lee Denmon III was gunned down in his parents' driveway earlier this year [2003], apparently mistaken by gangbangers for someone else. He wasn't killed by white supremacists or by a racist police officer: Police say he was killed by someone living in the same neighborhood, someone who looked like him.

No Reaction from the Black Community

Some leaders in the African American community reading this article may be unhappy with me, but I'm tired of being politically correct, because that has not helped the problem.

What has troubled me deeply since Denmon's murder in March is the community's reaction to it. There wasn't one. He was mourned by his family and friends, and then life went on.

Compare that with what happened during the summer of 2002, when an Inglewood police officer slammed an African American teenager onto the hood of his police car. Civil rights and political leaders from around the country immediately converged on Inglewood and demanded action. Ministers and politicians organized urgent town hall meetings, candlelight vigils were held and people from around the Southland marched, demanding swift action from the justice system.

What gives? It's not that I condone police violence, but how can we be so alarmed when a white officer appears to have abused a black teenager and so nonchalant about the routine killing of young black males by other young black males? Just imagine the reaction if Denmon had been murdered by a white skinhead.

California just recalled its governor [Gray Davis] because he misled voters about the size of the budget deficit, reacted too slowly to the energy crisis, tripled the state's car tax and had all the personality of a spit wad. The recall rage captured the attention of the masses, the media followed, and before you could spell terminator, the recall qualified, an election was held and Gov. Gray Davis was thrown out of office.[1] How can we generate that kind of rage about violence in the African American community?

Protesters in Inglewood, California, demonstrate against police brutality that occurred in 2002. Some commentators argue that the African American community should express the same level of outrage at black-on-black gang violence.

The violence is so prevalent that I have young African American male students arriving late to my Tuesday evening class at Southwest College because their parents won't let them walk to school or take the bus through gang-plagued neighborhoods. If white college kids in Westwood could not walk to their evening classes at UCLA because of neighborhood violence, there would be immediate action.

A Blueprint for Action Is Needed

If someone as obscure as anti-tax advocate Ted Costa could lead a movement to bring down the governor of California, imagine the possibilities if African American leadership got together for a weekend summit with one agenda item: black-on-black crime and what to do about it.

Now, I understand that our community, like all communities, has its differences. Baptists disagree with Methodists, younger activists disagree with traditional civil rights groups, business folks disagree with community groups. Our political leaders are often at odds with one another. But the violence is so great and the loss of life so significant that we all need to set aside our differences and focus on solutions.

I know it's considered inappropriate to air dirty laundry outside the neighborhood, but silence is not stopping the mayhem. It's time to quit blaming everybody else for the problems of violence in our communities. We need churches to launch a crusade to discuss individual responsibility. We need parents to be more involved with their children and talk with them from an early age about respecting their communities. We need to identify gang members willing to give up that lifestyle and help them reform. But any gangbangers unwilling to stop the violence and death need to be removed from the community.

A weekend summit before the end of the year with civil-rights, religious, political and community leaders dedicated to starting a move-

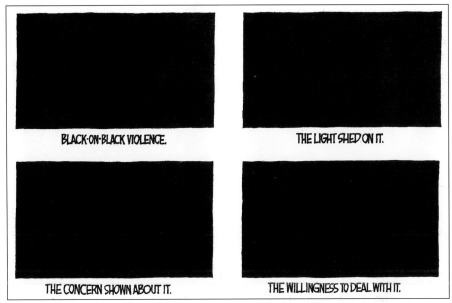

BLACK-ON-BLACK VIOLENCE.

THE LIGHT SHED ON IT.

THE CONCERN SHOWN ABOUT IT.

THE WILLINGNESS TO DEAL WITH IT.

Source: Borgman. © 1995 by the *Blade Citizen*. Reproduced by permission of King Features Syndicate.

ment to stop the violence in our communities would be a great way to start. The summit needs to focus specifically on what our leaders in Washington—working in concert with officials in Sacramento and with local leaders in Inglewood, Compton and Los Angeles—can do about stopping the violence.

There are already many individuals and groups working night and day to stop gang violence in their neighborhoods, including Khalid Shah of Stop the Violence, Increase the Peace and gang counselors Ed Turley and Perry Crouch. They're doing important work. But they need our help in putting their efforts in a bigger context, making them part of a broad movement supported by residents and leaders in affected communities.

What we need now is a comprehensive blueprint for action that goes far beyond press conferences, rallies, candlelight vigils and weekend marches. We've had all of those, but the problems remain.

Folks will volunteer by the hundreds if the effort appears serious and organized. We just need the leadership to make this a priority. We need people to take the lead, to make the calls, to take the risk. If our current leaders are unwilling to make this the top priority, then we need to reevaluate our leaders. If we can throw out a governor over a car tax, we ought to be able to get rid of people who continue to ignore slaughter in their communities.

Members of the east L.A. gang TMC visit the gravesite of a fellow gang member, who was killed by a rival gang.

A National Problem

This is not just a local problem. I recently spent a weekend in South Bend, Ind., where I saw the Notre Dame-USC football game. It seemed like a great way to escape briefly from urban America, and as an alumnus of USC, I was feeling pretty good on Saturday night about the whipping my team gave its archrival.

I woke up Sunday morning still glowing. But, as I was reading the *Chicago Tribune,* reality intervened. The paper featured the story of a college-bound Eritrean student senselessly murdered on the West Side of Chicago. Another black-on-black murder.

Los Angeles often leads the county in one trend or another. Wouldn't it be wonderful if the trend we exported this time involved solutions rather than problems? It will require action. Will someone organize the weekend summit or something like it before we lose another innocent 12-year-old walking out of church on a Sunday morning?

QUESTIONS FOR DISCUSSION:

The viewpoint you just read emphasizes the importance of community organizations such as churches and violence prevention programs in stopping gang violence. Think back to the first viewpoint in this chapter, by the *Syracuse Post-Standard*. Do you think the authors of that viewpoint would agree with Maddox? Why or why not?

FACTS ABOUT GANGS

According to the Office of Juvenile Justice and Delinquency Prevention, a Division of the Department of Justice, a Gang Must Have the Following Characteristics:

- A group of three or more members
- Members fall within a limited age range, usually 18 to 24
- Members have a shared sense of identity that is communicated through their name, hand signs, and clothing colors and styles
- The group must be stable, lasting at least a year
- The group is involved in criminal activity

The Extent of Gangs:

- Number of gangs in the United States in 2002: 21,500
- Number of gang members in the United States in 2002: 731,500
- The number of gang members decreased 32 percent between 1996 and 2002
- The decrease in gang members is due mostly to the decline of gang activity in small cities and rural areas
- Eighty-five percent of gang members are found in large cities and suburban counties

The Proportion of Youths Who Join Gangs:

- In a study of 6,000 eight-graders in eleven cities, 11 percent said they were currently gang members; 17 percent said they had belonged to a gang at some point
- In large cities, 14 to 30 percent of youths are gang members
- One-half to two-thirds of youths who join a gang remain in the gang for less than one year

The Extent of Gang-Related Homicides:

- Number of gang-related homicides in the United States in 2002: 1,232
- Number of gang-related homicides in Los Angeles and Chicago in 2002: 655

- Proportion of homicides in Los Angeles and Chicago that were gang-related in 2002: One-half

Police Perception of the Youth Gang Problem:
- Percentage of police officials who believe the gang problem is getting worse: 42%
- Percentage of police officials who believe the gang problem is getting better: 16%

The Ethnic Makeup of Gang Members in the United States:
- Latino: 49%
- African American: 34%
- White: 10%
- Asian: 6%
- Other: 1%

Percentage of Violent Crime That Can Be Attributed to Gang Members (According to One Study):
- Rochester, New York: 68%
- Seattle, Washington: 85%
- Denver, Colorado: 79%

Reasons Commonly Cited for Why Young People Join Gangs:
- An unfulfilling family situation leads them to seek a surrogate family in a gang
- Family tradition of gang membership
- The allure of excitement
- The need for protection
- To make money through crimes such as drug dealing and theft
- To gain respect
- To become more attractive to members of the opposite sex
- Peer pressure
- Boredom
- A lack of perceived alternatives such as school and work opportunities

The History of Gangs in the United States:
- The first U.S. gangs sprang up in New York and Philadelphia in the nineteenth century. They were formed by immigrant groups,

most notably the Irish, Germans, and Italians, the latter of whom formed the Mafia.

- By the twentieth century, numerous ethnic groups had gangs of their own, including Jews, Chinese, Poles, Slavs, blacks, and Mexicans.
- Youth gangs began to form after World War II due to the emergence of a youth subculture.
- The Crips and the Bloods are the two major black gangs of Los Angeles. The Crips emerged in the late 1960s, and the Bloods, their major rivals, emerged soon thereafter. Offshoots of the Crips can be found in most major cities nationwide. An offshoot of the Bloods can be found in New York City.
- The Norteños (also known as the Nuestra Familia, or "Our Family") and Sureños (also known as the Mexican Mafia) and are the two major Hispanic gangs of California. They are rivals who are centered in the northern and southern parts of the state, respectively.
- The Black Gangster Disciples, the Vice Lords, and the Latin Counts are the major gangs of Chicago. Branches of the Gangster Disciples are located in the cities of the East Coast.
- The Latin Kings, a Hispanic gang, emerged in Chicago in the 1960s and is now present in both Chicago and New York.
- The 1980s saw the rise of Latin American gangs, including the notoriously violent Mara Salvatrucha, or MS-13, a Salvadoran gang.
- Also in the 1980s, more Asian gangs began to form, including Vietnamese, Cambodian, and Laotian gangs.
- The Aryan Brotherhood is a white prison gang.

Signs That a Young Person May Be Involved in a Gang:
- Withdraws from family
- Shows intense need for secrecy
- Has sudden change in behavior or drop in grades at school
- Breaks rules at home and at school
- Wears gang clothing such as baggy pants, clothes of a particular color, and jewelry
- Has unexplained cash or goods such as jewelry or clothing
- Associates with gang members
- Gets gang tattoos or branding
- Shows obsession with gangster-influenced music and videos
- Draws gang graffiti in bedroom or on books, clothing, or shoes
- Uses hand signs to communicate with others
- Uses gang-style language

ORGANIZATIONS TO CONTACT

The editors have compiled the following list of organizations concerned with the issues debated in this book. The descriptions are derived from materials provided by the organizations. All have publications or information available for interested readers. The list was compiled on the date of publication of the present volume; the information provided here may change. Be aware that many organizations take several weeks or longer to respond to inquiries, so allow as much time as possible.

American Civil Liberties Union (ACLU)
125 Broad St., 18th Fl., New York, NY 10004
(212) 549-2500
fax: (212) 549-2646
e-mail: aclu@aclu.org
Web site: www.aclu.org

The ACLU is a national organization that works to defend Americans' civil rights as guaranteed by the U.S. Constitution. It opposes curfew laws for juveniles and others and seeks to protect the public-assembly rights of gang members or people associated with gangs. The ACLU publishes the biannual newsletter *Civil Liberties*.

Boys and Girls Clubs of America
1230 W. Peachtree St. NW, Atlanta, GA 30309
(404) 487-5700
e-mail: info@bgca.org
Web site: www.bgca.org

Boys and Girls Clubs of America supports juvenile gang prevention programs in its individual clubs throughout the United States. The organization's Targeted Outreach Delinquency Prevention program relies on referrals from schools, courts, law enforcement, and youth service agencies to recruit at-risk youths into ongoing club programs and activities. The clubs publish *Gang Prevention Through Targeted Outreach*, a manual designed to assist local clubs in reaching youngsters before they become involved in gang activity.

Center for the Study and Prevention of Violence (CSPV)
Institute of Behavioral Science, University of Colorado at Boulder
Campus Box 439, Boulder, CO 80309-0439
(303) 492-8465
fax: (303) 443-3297
e-mail: cspv@colorado.edu
Web site: www.colorado.edu/cspv

The CSPV was founded in 1992 to provide information and assistance to organizations that are dedicated to preventing violence, particularly youth violence. Its publications include the paper "Gangs and Adolescent Violence," and the fact sheets "Gangs and Youth Violence" and "Female Juvenile Violence."

Child Welfare League of America (CWLA)
440 First St. NW, 3rd Floor, Washington, DC 20001-2085
(202) 638-2952
fax: (202) 638-4004
Web site: www.cwla.org

The Child Welfare League of America, a social welfare organization concerned with setting standards for welfare and human services agencies, works to improve care and services for abused, dependent, or neglected children, youth, and their families. It publishes information on gangs and youth crime in the bimonthly journal *Child Welfare* as well as in several books, including *Beating the Odds: Crime, Poverty, and Life in the Inner City* and *Girls in the Juvenile Justice System.*

John Howard Society of Alberta
2nd Floor, 10523-100 Ave., Edmonton, AB T5J 0A8 Canada
(780) 423-4878
fax: (780) 425-0008
e-mail: info@johnhoward.ab.ca
Web site: www.johnhoward.ab.ca

The John Howard Society of Alberta is a nonprofit agency concerned with the problem of crime and its prevention, and works to encourage people in the community to play an active role in the criminal justice process. Its publications include the newsletter the *Reporter* and various reports and papers including *Gangs* and *Youth Crime in Canada: Public Perception vs. Statistical Information.*

National Gang Crime Research Center (NGCRC)
PO Box 990, Peotone, IL 60468-0990
(708) 258-9111
fax: (708) 258-9546
e-mail: gangcrime@aol.com
Web site: www.ngcrc.com

The NGCRC is a nonprofit, independent agency that conducts research on gangs and gang members and disseminates information through publications and reports. It publishes the *Journal of Gang Research.*

National Major Gang Task Force (NMGTF)
338 S. Arlington Ave., Suite 112, Indianapolis, IN 46219
(317) 322-0537
fax: (317) 322-0549
e-mail: nmgtf@earthlink.net
Web site: www.nmgtf.org

The NMGTF's goal is to provide a centralized link for all fifty state correctional systems, the Federal Bureau of Prisons, major jails, law enforcement, and probation and parole officers throughout the nation. The task force accomplishes this mission by generating and maintaining the National Correction Informational Sharing System, which is available to gang prevention groups across the country. It publishes the monograph "From the Street to the Prison: Understanding and Responding to Gangs."

National School Safety Center (NSSC)
141 Duesenberg Dr., Suite 11, Westlake Village, CA 91362
(805) 373-9977
fax: (805) 373-9277
e-mail: info@nssc1.org
Web site: www.nssc1.org

Part of Pepperdine University, the center is a research organization that studies school crime and violence, including gang and hate crimes, and that provides technical assistance to local school systems. NSSC believes that teacher training is an effective means of reducing these problems. Its publications include the book *Gangs in Schools: Breaking Up Is Hard to Do* and the *School Safety Update* newsletter.

National Youth Gang Center (NYGC)
Institute for Intergovernmental Research
PO Box 12729, Tallahassee, FL 32317
(850) 385-0600
fax: (850) 386-5356
e-mail: nygc@iir.com
Web site: www.iir.com/nygc

The National Youth Gang Center was developed by the Office of Juvenile Justice and Delinquency Prevention (OJJDP) to collect, analyze, and distribute information on gangs and gang-related legislation, research, and programs. Its publications include *The NYGC Bibliography of Gang Literature*. It also makes numerous gang-related articles accessible on its Web site and on *OJJDP's Gang Publication,* a CD-ROM that it distributes on request.

Office of Juvenile Justice and Delinquency Prevention (OJJDP)
810 Seventh St. NW, Washington, DC 20531
(202) 307-5911
fax: (202) 307-2093
Web site: http://ojjdp.ncjrs.org

As the primary federal agency charged with monitoring and improving the juvenile justice system, the OJJDP develops and funds programs on juvenile justice. Through its Juvenile Justice Clearinghouse, the OJJDP distributes fact sheets, the annual *National Youth Gang Survey,* and reports such as "Youth Gangs: An Overview" and "Gang Suppression and Intervention: Community Models."

Teens Against Gang Violence (TAGV)
1486 Dorchester Ave., Dorchester, MA 02124
(617) 825-8248
e-mail: teensagv@aol.com
Web site: www.tagv.org

Teens Against Gang Violence is a volunteer, community-based, teen peer leadership program. TAGV distinguishes between gangs that are nonviolent and those that participate in violence. Through presentations and workshops, the organization educates teens, parents, schools, and community groups on violence, guns, and drug prevention. It provides information about its programs on its Web site.

FOR FURTHER READING

Books

Herbert C. Covey, *Street Gangs Throughout the World.* Springfield, IL: Charles C. Thomas, 2003. A summary of research on gangs worldwide with an emphasis on characteristics shared by all gangs regardless of nationality, ethnicity, or gender.

G. David Curry and Scott H. Decker, *Confronting Gangs: Crime and Community.* Los Angeles: Roxbury Park, 2002. Summarizes recent research and policy findings on gangs, with chapters on gang-related crime, female gang involvement, and solutions to gang-related violence.

Sean Donahue, ed., *Gangs: Stories of Life and Death from the Streets.* New York: Thunder's Mouth, 2002. An anthology of fiction, nonfiction, and journalistic accounts of gangs of the past and present.

Maureen P. Duffy and Scott Edward Gillig, eds., *Teen Gangs: A Global View.* Westport, CT: Greenwood, 2004. An anthology of essays that describe the nature and extent of gang culture in different parts of the world, including Europe, Asia, the Caribbean, Latin America, and Asia.

Finn-Aage Esbensen, Stephen G. Tibbetts, and Larry Gaines, *American Youth Gangs at the Millennium.* Long Grove, IL: Waveland, 2004. A team of scholars and researchers address the status of youth gangs in America at the turn of the twenty-first century with a focus on specific issues, including the risk factors of joining a gang and community responses to gang violence.

Arnold P. Goldstein and Donald W. Kodluboy, *Gangs in Schools: Signs, Symbols, and Solutions.* Champaign, IL: Research Press, 1998. Outlines methods for recognizing, intervening, and preventing gang activity in schools and describes attractive school-based alternatives to gang membership in order to maximize school safety.

C. Ronald Huff, ed., *Gangs in America III.* Thousand Oaks, CA: Sage, 2002. The third edition of an anthology that examines contemporary gangs and community and law enforcement responses to them.

Essays include discussions of girl gangs and the connections between gangs, drugs, and guns.

Malcolm W. Klein, *The American Street Gang: Its Nature, Prevalence, and Control.* New York: Oxford University Press, 1995. A scholarly discussion of gangs that focuses in part on the nature and prevalence of gang violence.

Louis Kontos, David Brotherton, and Luis Barrios, eds., *Gangs and Society: Alternative Perspectives.* New York: Columbia University Press, 2003. An anthology of essays that examine various aspects of gangs, including political and legal issues related to gangs, women in gangs, and gang photography.

Richard C. McCorkle and Terance D. Miethe, *Panic: The Social Construction of the Street Gang Problem.* Upper Saddle River, NJ: Prentice-Hall, 2002. Two criminologists argue that gangs emerged as a social problem not due to an increase in gang activity, but rather due to the exaggerated claims of law enforcement officials, the media, and the academic community.

Jodie Miller, *One of the Guys: Girls, Gangs, and Gender.* New York: Oxford University Press, 2001. A study of girls' involvement in gangs that examines why girls join gangs, the nature of girls' involvement in gangs, and how gang membership leads to violence and victimization for girls. It includes interviews with girl gang members.

Marie Miranda, *Homegirls in the Public Sphere.* Austin: University of Texas Press, 2003. An anthropological look at girl gangs in Oakland, California, that challenges the popular conception of such gangs.

Randall G. Sheldon, Sharon K. Tracy, and William B. Brown, *Youth Gangs in American Society.* Belmont, CA: Wadsworth, 2001. Presents the latest research on the history and development of gangs, the different types of gangs and gang activity, and antigang strategies.

Irving A. Spergel, *The Youth Gang Problem: A Community Approach.* New York: Oxford University Press, 1995. An in-depth analysis of gangs that challenges the common assumptions regarding the relationship between gangs, drug trafficking, and gang violence.

Gini Sikes, *8 Ball Chicks.* New York: Doubleday, 1997. An examination of girl gangs in several U.S. cities by a seasoned journalist who spent a year among them.

George Tita et al., *Reducing Gun Violence: Results from an Intervention in East Los Angeles.* Santa Monica, CA: Rand, 2003. A report on an intervention to reduce gang violence in East Los Angeles by means of increased police presence and stricter enforcement of housing codes and gun laws.

Raúl Damacio Tovares, *Manfacturing the Gang: Mexican American Youth Gangs on Local Television News.* Westport, CT: Greenwood, 2002. The author studied the portrayal of Mexican American youth gangs on local television news in Austin, Texas. He concludes that a lack of professionalism and fairness among journalists results in distorted coverage that reinforces negative stereotypes of Latinos as violence-prone criminals.

James Diego Vigil, *A Rainbow of Gangs: Street Cultures in the Mega-City.* Austin: University of Texas Press, 2002. A study of Chicano, African American, Vietnamese, and Salvadoran gangs in Los Angeles. The author illustrates his analysis by presenting the life stories of actual gang members.

Valerie Wiener, *Winning the War Against Youth Gangs: A Guide for Teens, Families, and Communities.* Westport, CT: Greenwood, 1999. An overview of the characteristics of youth gangs and approaches to preventing young people from joining them. The text is peppered with quotes from interviews with adolescents reflecting on their experiences with gangs.

Lewis Yablonsky, *Gangsters: Fifty Years of Madness, Drugs, and Death on the Streets of America.* New York: New York University Press, 1997. A criminologist explores why young people join gangs, the nature of gang life, and recommended approaches to prevent gang violence.

Periodicals and Reports

David Allender, "Gangs in Middle America: Are They a Threat?" *FBI Law Enforcement Bulletin,* December 2001.

American Correctional Association, "Gangs Inside," *Corrections Compendium,* April 2000.

Beth Barrett, "Bratton's Challenge: LAPD's New Chief Believes Gang Problem Can Be Solved," *Los Angeles Daily News,* October 2, 2004.

———, "Homegrown Terror," *Los Angeles Daily News,* September 26, 2004.

Jonathan Bartholomew, "The Gangbuster," *Reader's Digest,* November 2002.

Vince Beiser, "Boyz on the Rez," *New Republic,* July 10, 2000.

Leon Bing, "Homegirls," *Rolling Stone,* April 12, 2001.

Gregory J. Boyle, "Gang Bill Panders to Irrational Fear; the Problem Is Social, Not a Matter for Law Enforcement," *Los Angeles Times,* December 18, 2003.

———, "A Lethal Absence of Hope," *Los Angeles Times,* October 15, 2002.

———, "The Mythic Enemy," *Los Angeles Times,* December 15, 2002.

Matthew Brzezinski, "Hillbangers," *New York Times Magazine,* August 15, 2004.

California Attorney General's Office, Crime and Violence Prevention Center, *Gangs: A Community Response,* June 2003.

Terry Carter, "'Equality with a Vengeance': Violent Crimes and Gang Activity by Girls Skyrocket," *ABA Journal,* November 1999.

Congressional Digest, "Loitering and Individual Rights," *Supreme Court Debates,* February 1999.

Terry Costlow, "A Town Fights Gangs by Obtaining Right to Sue Them," *Christian Science Monitor,* May 20, 2002.

Kelly Creedon, "El Salvador: War on Gangs," *NACLA Report on the Americas,* November/December 2003.

Donna De Cesare, "Dangerous Exile: More than 400,000 Noncitizens Have Been Deported Since 1996 Because of Expanded Criminal Sentencing," *Colorlines,* Fall 2003.

Economist, "The Trouble with Gangs," January 16, 1999.

———, "Wild Things: Gangs," May 4, 2002.

Catherine Edwards, "When Girl Power Goes Gangsta," *Insight,* March 20, 2000.

James Emery, "Misplaced Loyalty: Asian Gangs Lure Teens to a Life of Crime," *Denver Post,* August 20, 2000.

———, "Their World, Not Ours—Hmong Gangs in America," *World & I,* December 2002.

Susan Estrich, "Defining Criminal Behavior," *Liberal Opinion Week,* July 5, 1999.

Dianne Feinstein, "Congress Must Address Upsurge in Gangs," *Los Angeles Daily News,* March 10, 2004.

Mariel Garza, "War on Gangs: Getting Tough Just Isn't Enough," *Los Angeles Daily News,* December 7, 2003.

Jeff Glasser, "The Software Sopranos," *U.S. News & World Report,* February 7, 2000.

Heike P. Gramckow and Elena Tompkins, "Enabling Prosecutors to Address Drug, Gang, and Youth Violence," *JAIBG Bulletin,* December 1999.

Tom Hayden, "Gato and Alex—No Safe Place—Gangs and State Violence: The Human Story of the Los Angeles Police Scandal," *Nation,* July 10, 2000.

———, "The Truth Also Falls Victim to Gang Violence," *Los Angeles Times,* April 14, 2003.

Karl G. Hill, Christina Lui, and J. David Hawkins, "Early Precursors of Gang Membership: A Study of Seattle Youth," *Juvenile Justice Bulletin,* December 2001.

James C. Howell, Arlen Egley Jr., and Debra K. Gleason, "Modern Day Youth Gangs," *Juvenile Justice Bulletin,* June 2002.

James C. Howell and Debra K. Gleason, "Youth Gang Drug Trafficking," *Juvenile Justice Bulletin,* December 1999.

Indian Country Today, "Violence or Hope: Choose Your Path," February 18, 2004.

Issues & Controversies, "Teen Gangs," May 12, 2000.

Lonnie Jackson, "Understanding and Responding to Youth Gangs: A Juvenile Corrections Approach," *Corrections Today,* August 1999.

Ember Reichgott Junge, "Assistant U.S. Attorney Works to Prosecute Gangs, Leaders," *Minnesota Lawyer,* January 27, 2003.

Karen Kaplan, "Gangs Finding New Turf," *Los Angeles Times,* May 31, 2001.

Jill Leovy, "Mortal Wounds," *Los Angeles Times,* November 18, 2003.

Marcy Levin-Epstein, ed., "Rise in Gang Activity Suspected," *Inside School Safety,* January 2004.

Bill Lockyer, "Blueprint to Reduce Youth Gang Violence," *Business Journal,* May 2, 2003.

Aline K. Major et al., "Youth Gangs in Indian Country," *Juvenile Justice Bulletin,* March 2004.

Terry McCarthy, "The Gang Buster," *Time,* January 19, 2004.

John McCormick, "Winning a Gang War," *Newsweek,* November 1, 1999.

Sarah McNaught, "Gangsta Girls," *Boston Phoenix,* May 20–27, 1999.

Kenneth Miller, "Out of the Crossfire," *People Weekly,* December 8, 2003.

O. Ricardo Pimentel, "Gang Injunctions Trample Some Basic Rights," *Arizona Republic,* June 13, 2000.

Kit R. Roane, Angie Cannon, and Mike Tharp, "Deadly Numbers: Cops Fear New Surge," *U.S. News & World Report,* February 26, 2001.

Luis J. Rodriguez, "Could Today's Ganghangers Be Tomorrow's Heroes?" *Los Angeles Times,* December 19, 2002.

Lawrence Rosenthal, "Gang Loitering and Race," *Journal of Criminal Law & Criminology,* Fall 2000.

Frank Salvato, "Gang Violence: The Ultimate Denial of Free Speech," *Washington Dispatch,* October 28, 2003.

Heather Slater, "Anti-Loitering Laws Asked to 'Move Along,'" *OpinionEditorials.com,* April 18, 2003.

David Starbuck, James C. Howell, and Donna J. Lindquist, "Hybrid and Other Modern Gangs," *Juvenile Justice Bulletin,* December 2001.

Jacob Sullum, "Sweeping Powers," *Reason,* October 14, 1998.

William Tiplett, "Gang Crisis," *CQ Researcher,* May 14, 2004.

Mark Totten, "Dispelling Myths About Youth Violence," *Ottawa Citizen,* February 10, 1999.

Joseph Trevino, "Politics in the Street: The Debate That Matters on Gang Injunctions," *LA Weekly,* May 25–31, 2001.

Paul Douglas White, "Freedom Is Never Risk-Free: Gangs Will Continue to Tyrannize If We Let Them," *Los Angeles Daily News,* September 14, 2003.

Daniel B. Wood, "As Gangs Rise, So Do Calls for U.S.-wide Dragnet," *Christian Science Monitor,* February 4, 2004.

Gary Yates, "New Thinking Can Help Defeat Gang Violence," *Los Angeles Times,* November 29, 2003.

Web Sites

The Coroner's Report (www.gangwar.com). The project of Steve Nawojczyk, a former coroner and a nationally recognized gang researcher, the Web site includes an overview of American gangs, information on gang graffiti, as well as other articles and links on youth gangs.

Into the Abyss: A Personal Journey into the World of Street Gangs (http://courses.smsu.edu/mkc096f/gangbook). This Web site maintained by sociologist Mike Carlie features the entire contents of his book *Into the Abyss* as well as additional articles, updates, and Web site links about street gangs.

National Alliance of Gang Investigators Associations (NAGIA) (www.nagia.org). This Web site is a creation of NAGIA, an organization of criminal justice professionals and organizations that works to promote and coordinate national antigang strategies. It includes an online library of articles and links to regional gang investigation organizations.

Streetgangs.com (www.streetgangs.com). This Web site, created and maintained by gang researcher Alejandro A. Alonso, a doctoral student of geography at the University of Southern California in Los Angeles, presents a history of gangs in Los Angeles. It is not intended to glamorize the street gang culture but to help parents, educators, and youth understand how and why the gang phenomena has become so persuasive. It includes news articles about gangs and an extensive bibliography of gang research.

INDEX

African Americans. *See* minorities
American Civil Liberties Union (ACLU), 90
antiloitering laws, 82–86, 90–92

Barrett, Beth, 56
Barrios, Jarrett, 90
Bosanko, Neil, 84
Breyer, Stephen, 86

Cavitt, Pete, 57, 62–63
Chesney-Lind, Meda, 24
Chicago Tribune (newspaper), 106
Chicago v. Morales (1999), 81, 82
cliques, 18, 19
clothes/jewelry, as sign of gang involvement, 97
Cohen, Mark A., 21
community involvement, 102–107
Costa, Ted, 104
crews, 18, 19
crime

violent, trends in, 20–22
see also gang violence
Crouch, Perry, 105

Davis, Gray, 102–103
Decker, Scott H., 94, 95
Denmon, Lee, 102
Department of Justice, U.S., 22
Driscoll, Matt, 75
drug trafficking, gangs and, 28, 33–34
DuVal, Dennis, 73, 75

Ellis, Charlene, 46
Ellis, Larry, 52
Evans, Paul, 90
Everson, Delmar, 52–53

family. *See* parents
female gang members, 17, 66
Fight Crime: Invest in Kids, 16
Fitzpatrick, William, 74, 75
Fox, James Alan, 17

PICTURE CREDITS

ABOUT THE EDITOR

Scott Barbour received a bachelor's degree in English and a master's degree in social work from San Diego State University. He has worked as a case manager and counselor with the severely mentally ill. He is currently a senior acquisitions editor for Greenhaven Press, for whom he has edited numerous books on social issues, historical topics, and current events.